SPIRITISM AND THE FALLEN ANGELS
IN THE LIGHT OF THE OLD AND NEW TESTAMENTS

JAMES MARTIN GRAY

ALICIA EDITIONS

CONTENTS

1. THE NEW ATTACK OF SPIRITUALISM AND HOW TO MEET IT	5
2. THE MODERN HISTORY OF SPIRITISM	10
3. SATAN—OR SPIRITISM AT ITS SOURCE	17
4. ANGELS AND DEMONS, OR SPIRITISM'S PERSONNEL	24
5. SPIRITISM BEFORE THE FLOOD	29
6. "SONS OF GOD" MARRYING THE "DAUGHTERS OF MEN"	36
7. ABOMINATIONS OF THE CANAANITES	42
8. SPIRITISM IN ISRAEL AND JUDAH	50
9. EARLY CHRISTIANITY AND THE BLACK ART	56
10. TEACHING OF THE PAULINE EPISTLES	63
11. TEACHING OF THE GENERAL EPISTLES	74
12. TEACHING OF THE APOCALYPSE	83

THE NEW ATTACK OF SPIRITUALISM AND HOW TO MEET IT

I

Of writing books on Spiritualism in these days there is no end. But with a single exception, and that rather inadequate in its treatment of the subject, we have found none to put into the hands of a Christian desirous of learning how to meet and deal with this error from an all round Biblical point of view.

Some were too technical, some too bulky and expensive and some so mixed with other error as to be impossible to recommend.

Not a few were written by those who were well-informed on the scientific phases of Spiritualism, the findings of the Society of Psychical Research or the doings of mediums and séances, but whose authors appeared either ignorant of or indifferent to the Bible, which to the Christian, of course, holds the first place and is of final authority.

Some of the writers were of the novelist type like Sir A. Conan Doyle, Basil King or Booth Tarkington, and antagonistic to Christianity considering it a confirmed failure. These referred to the Bible to ridicule its teachings or to wrest their meaning into conformity with their own views, being convinced, as one of them said, that Spiritualism is "not only a new religion but the coming religion."

We intended to briefly analyze some of these books for the sake of the warning they contain, but this has been so well done by the Sunday School Times in the case of Basil King's "*The Abolishing of Death*," that we take the liberty to quote. The reviewer confesses the masterful character of the work and the fact that it intelligently recognizes the fundamentals of the Christian faith, but, as he adds, it just as intelligently rejects them:

> "The unique inspiration of the Bible is rejected.
> The finality of the Bible's message, as a complete revelation from God for all men for this life, is rejected.
> The unique deity of Christ is rejected.
> The necessity for the blood atonement of Christ is rejected.
> The existence and reality of sin are rejected.
> God's word that some men will be lost and some will be saved is rejected.
> The reality of death is rejected.
> The need of faith in Christ as Saviour as a condition of eternal life is rejected.
> God's word as to hell, or the second death, is rejected.
> The lines between sin and holiness are obliterated.
> And the divinity of all men, which the Bible denies, is declared."

II

It is astonishing and saddening too, to read some of the arguments advanced in books and other writings on this subject, by Christian ministers, in their efforts to dissuade their flocks from following these false shepherds.

One warns them to beware of the medieval system of demonology, which on further investigation turns out to mean really Bible demonology. He would have his ministerial brethren also deny absolutely that a medium can receive communications from another world, because, he adds, "this would make it inconsistent to suggest that their communications were from evil spirits!" It seems almost impossible that such a man ever could have consulted his Bible except as he goes to a book of familiar quotations to select a text.

That mediums can receive communications from another world there is no doubt, nor is there any doubt that their communications are from evil spirits, for the Bible confirms both propositions. That is not to say, however, that all mediums receive such communications, nor that any medium receives them in every case, there are frauds perpetrated as every one knows; but in principle it is as. foolish to deny this as it is for an ostrich to hide its head in the sand and suppose that it can not be seen.

Another expresses the opinion that it is perfectly natural to seek communion with those we have loved and who have passed beyond, and that there is no reason why we should not talk with them if they are near to us; but advises against it because "the means of communication and the machinery of contact is as yet so imperfect!" In other words, as soon as scientists have perfected the apparatus, communications between the living and the dead, may be popularized, not merely without harm to any but with positive benefit to all. It is like the aeroplane which will soon lose its interest for sportsmen and scientists and become a common carrier.

Strange to say, this last opinion is from a writer of the Evangelical type apparently, for he goes on to say that while such intercourse with the dead would be a great comfort and a renewed assurance of the persistence of life after death, yet after all that is not religion. "Religion," he truly witnesses, "is the consciousness of God, the sense of redemption from sin through Jesus Christ, joy and peace in the Holy Ghost, service of the world, and love and tenderness for all mankind." One wonders that a man so intelligent in the Gospel could possibly be led into folly of this kind and into such gross contradiction of the Bible. It may be natural enough for us to seek communion with our departed, but the reason we should refrain from it is because God has forbidden it. What further do we need?

Perhaps as confusing as anything we have seen was a review of four new books, in an English evangelical periodical, in which the claims and teachings of Spiritualism were weighed in the balance and found wanting, and as to which the reviewer said he heartily commended them all. Two of these books were thoroughly sound and Biblical in their contention, but one of the others was that referred to above as containing the theory that mediums could have no intercourse with demons, and the fourth advocated, as an offset to Spiritualism, that Christians give more diligence in intercession of the saints and prayers for the dead!

The reviewer would explain his inconsistency doubtless, by the circumstance that all agreed in teaching that between Spiritualism and Christianity there was no affinity. Nevertheless, if such lack of discrimination were everywhere, we could well appreciate the remark of another Englishman that "the word 'Christianity' has undergone such enlargement that I scarcely know what it means when I see it."

III

Speaking further of the inability and lack of Biblical knowledge in dealing with this subject on the part of some who ought to be 'teachers in Israel', it recalls the situation when Christian Science first raised its head as an avowed rival of the Church and when, as a result, the ministry was thrown into a panic.

And by the way, the editor of Christian Work on his return from England not long since, reported that now one seldom heard Christian Science referred to there. The war, he said, had dissipated all illusions as to the non-existence of evil, and to quote his words, "men who have been buried under a shower of legs, arms, heads and mutilated trunks of human bodies falling all about them do not make easy converts to that faith. But everybody is talking about Spiritualism," he went on to say, "and spiritualistic meetings are being held all over the country, and there are séances on every street. So alarmed have the churches become that the preachers are delivering sermons regarding it, and the religious press is printing weekly editorials."

It was the same in this country and especially in and around Boston, where the present writer lived in the early eighties, which saw the rise and development of Mrs. Eddy's delusion. Of course it was the proper thing to deliver sermons and write editorials against it if only they aimed straight and used the right ammunition; but pastors and church committees, not a few, were ready to capitulate or compromise after the first campaign, and to admit the validity of Christian Science as a church and grant letters dimissory to it.

We remember that Dr. A. J. Gordon was proclaimed a saviour when, in an issue of the Congregationalist of April 1885, he contributed an article, later circulated by the thousands in leaflet form, entitled, "Christian Science Tested by Scripture." Everybody thought Scripture should be recognized in the premises and that its dictum would settle the matter at least for believers, but until Dr. Gordon rose up to say the word, no one else seemed able or willing to go about it.

History is repeating itself, but while many like the Hebrews with Saul at Gilgal, are going "over Jordan to the land of Gad and Gilead," not a few are remaining true and with trumpets of no uncertain sound proclaiming a "Thus saith the Lord."

We are happy to join their number, and at the request of our publisher, to do what we can in the chapters of this book to aid Christians in understanding and meeting the error of Spiritualism from the Bible point of view.

THE MODERN HISTORY OF SPIRITISM

I

Spiritualism at its source is older than man, but we have no intention of tracing it to its source just now, that will come later. At the moment we wish to deal with it only for the period of time during which it has been known by its present name.

And yet its present name is not the best because it has too wide an application. At one time "Spiritualism" was used to designate the doctrines and religious life of mystics like Jacob Bohme and Madame Guyon who tried to live consecrated lives subject to the Holy Spirit, and in obedience to the Word of God.

As a French investigator put it, "spiritualism is the opposite of materialism. Whoever believes he has something within him distinguished from matter is a spiritualist," in which sense, of course, all true Christians are spiritualists, though it does not follow that they practice communications with spirits of an invisible world.

Therefore to designate this latter belief the word "Spiritism" has come to be used, which we shall employ hereafter, meaning by it the idea of some people, that the living can and do communicate with the spirits of the departed, and also including the various practices resorted to in that intercourse.

II

Spiritism, which is also necromancy or the evocation of the dead, was a feature of that Gnosticism which assailed the Christian Church in the Apostolic era, and against which Paul, by the Holy Spirit, inveighs particularly in his epistle to the Colossians. And this, in turn, indicates that it was not a new thing even then, but that it formed a part of the earlier pagan religions. Allusions to it have been found in Homer, Strabo ascribes its practice to the early Persians, Theodoret finds it in Chaldea and Babylonia, and readers of the Old Testament recall Moses speaking of it as among the abominations of the Canaanites (Deut. XVIII) of which we speak in a later chapter.

The Delphic oracles (more than 600 B. C.) are claimed by Spiritists and we believe with good reason, and the same may be said of the lives of seers and clairvoyants and the facts of witchcraft in all ages. "Never would that oracle at Delphi have been so celebrated nor stored with so many gifts from all kinds of peoples and kings, unless every age had experienced the truth of its utterances" (Cicero, De Divinatione 19).

To come to the Christian period, the early Church fathers assume as unquestionable the agency of evil spirits in the pagan oracles and rites, showing themselves by divinations, cures and dreams. The records of the Roman Catholic Church also speak of phenomena which bear a close resemblance to present-day Spiritism. During the Reformation Luther published a treatise against "The Celestial Prophets", so-called, of Germany, whom he charged with exercising the imitative powers of Satan.

There were occurrences in the Wesley family ascribed to Spiritism (1716), and it is commonly believed to explain much in Swedenborg's alleged full and open communication with the spirit world.

In America, David Brainerd, in his work among the Indians, declared that one of his greatest difficulties was the conviction they held that their diviners had supernatural power, a conviction he himself shared.

In 1843, the Shakers at New Lebanon, N. Y., became the subjects of strange experiences, and influences purporting to be spirits who had lived in the world in different ages, took possession of their bodies and spoke through their vocal organs.

III

What is known as the "spirit-rapping" phenomenon began in March, 1848, in the family of John D. Fox in Hydeville, N. Y., whose daughters a few years afterwards began to give public performances.

The alleged spiritist manifestations of these young women became the subject of extensive newspaper discussion with the result that "mediums", through whom they were said to occur, were multiplied in different parts of the country by hundreds and thousands.

The séances of the Fox girls before the Civil War were attended by some of the most prominent men of the country, and when they visited Europe they had the nobility and royalty for their auditors. Societies were organized, and disciples and imitators came forward in great numbers.

IV

This brings us to the scientific epoch in Spiritism, when such men as Sir William Crookes, the English chemist and physicist, who died recently, became actively interested in it.

In the London Quarterly Journal of January, 1874, he classified the phenomena under some ten or a dozen heads, and also conducted exhibitions in his own house, mostly in the light, when it is said that the existence of an unexplained force was accurately tested by means of an ingenious apparatus.

In other words, with Sir William Crookes' investigations it began to be felt that the phenomena of Spiritism were not all fraud, and while the scientists were unable to explain the source of some of them, their ignorance in the premises went so far to confirm the teaching of the Bible that the source was to be found in the superhuman realm.

Sir William testified that "it was a common thing for seven or eight of us in the laboratory to see Miss Cook (the medium) and 'Katie' (the spirit) at the same time under the full blaze of the electric light." On one occasion, the electrician showed to the satisfaction of the spectators that the medium was inside the cabinet while the supposed spirit form was visible and moving outside.

Quoting Nelson's Encyclopædia, it was the organization of the Society of Psychical Research (England, 1882; America, 1888) that revived recent interest in the doctrine. Its work has tended to put limits to the claims which have been made for communication with the discarnate, though it has at the same time strengthened the belief in it by giving it better scientific credentials. Reports on the remarkable case of Mrs. Piper were published in five different volumes of the Proceedings of this Society, and it is said that they offer the best mass of scientific evidence extant in support of possible spirit communication.

It was the evidence derived from this woman's case when she crossed the Atlantic in 1889, that finally convinced Sir Oliver Lodge that deceased relatives spoke or sent messages through her organism informing him both of known and unknown facts subsequently verified. In other words, to quote him exactly, it convinced him "that the brain and organism of a living person might be utilized by deceased personalities whose own bodies had ceased to work."

To avoid an erroneous supposition in the light of some things which we have already said, let it be stated clearly at this point that the Bible is against the conclusion of Sir Oliver. It reveals, as we shall subsequently discover, the possibility of materializations, but not the actual talking with the dead. By materialization in this case we mean the assumption of a material and bodily form by evil angels or demons who wickedly personate the dead and deceive the living, but nothing more. The proof of this will follow, but to avoid any possible misunderstanding at the outset, the fact itself is here stated.

V

The current revival of Spiritism, or "the Spiritist intrusion", as *Life* called it, dates from the recent war, and was predicted by close and earnest students of the Bible. It is "due to the bereavements of the war and to the longing of broken hearts to find out something concerning the destiny of those who have been taken from them." Instead of turning "to the law and to the testimony" as the inspired prophet exhorts, they have taken up with spirits "that peep and that mutter" (Isaiah VIII. 19, 20).

"There is hardly a home in England," we are told, "from which some boy has not gone forever during these last two years. Can they be reached? Can one have communion with them? Can they break through the wall between their world and ours?

"Then, one by one, such men as Sir Oliver Lodge and Sir A. Conan Doyle published books saying, 'We have had communications from our boys, and have spoken with them and with their comrades who perished on the field of battle.'

"Thousands of parents responded, 'If they, why not we?' And the result has been an almost overwhelming rush to mediums, and long lists of séances are now advertised in the papers." (Editorial in The Christian Work).

In our opinion the campaign of the powers of darkness gained its greatest headway up until that date during the fighting from Mons to Ypres.

Readers will recall a fantastic story of that period published at first in a London evening paper, and entitled, "The Bowman", which purported to tell how St. George and the old Agincourt bowmen appeared during the retreat from Mons and fought with the British against the foe. The author frankly declared it was pure fiction, but so heated was the British imagination at the time and so psychologically ready for the reception of the occult, that he was not believed by many who seriously entertained the opinion that angels appeared to the soldiers.

Nor were these in all cases the intellectually weak, but in some instances intelligent and educated men and women, including a Christian scholar whom we personally know, and who is honored throughout Christendom. Indeed an eminent clergyman of London is reported to have said that such a case of spiritual intervention was "eminently creditable. Joan of Arc saved her country owing to the vision of an angel, and why should not the phenomenon be repeated in this case?"

Immediately people began to hold intercourse with their beloved dead, as was supposed. The Christian scholar, in a private letter to the writer, said: "My wife saw her boy in his spiritual body permitted to come once to comfort her. We know. It is the same with many. This war is given for the convincing of many that the future life is a real thing, and that God Himself speaks to man. This is the one consolation that remains out of this hideous and horrible time of trial. My wife was permitted to talk to her boy. He was even more radiant than in life, but otherwise the same. He told her of his death and the manner of it. We learned after a month that this was true. Some people call it a dream. I know it was a vision granted to soothe her sorrow and her longing. This has nothing to do with magic. The spiritual eye saw the spiritual body."

VI

It would not be the part of wisdom for the writer to delay warning the unwary until our consideration of this subject approached its conclusion. Hence a pause is made here to say that the experiences above recorded are very different from those of Bible saints.

Let a brief reference be made again to Isaiah's words (VIII. 19-22). He sees Israel in the latter days in great distress, doubtless far beyond anything known in the late war. They are "hardly bestead and hungry", "behold trouble, darkness, dimness of anguish". "They are seeking "unto them that have familiar spirits and unto wizards that peep and that mutter", and he rebukes them, saying, "Should not a people seek unto their God? On behalf of the living should they seek unto the dead? To the law and to the testimony; if they speak not according to this word, it is because there is no light in them."

In other words, are not the Word and the Spirit of God the source, and the sufficient source, of the Christian's comfort in this age? Does he need such visions to convince him of the future life and that God speaks to men? The rich man in our Lord's story in Luke 16 thought well of that kind of evidence, but we remember how fruitless "father Abraham" thought it would be. If such things are the only, or the strongest, consolation remaining for God's people in such a time of trial, what of the millions of them to whom they do not come?

Let the Christian ever keep in mind that there are such beings as evil spirits, of whom we shall learn considerable by and by, and let him consider further that fundamentally only these are in evidence in this modern outbreak of Spiritism.

In proof of this it may be mentioned that in all the accounts of the angels at Mons which came to our attention, not once was Jesus Christ so much as named. St. George was named, and Joan of Arc, and Socrates, and Swedenborg, and the Virgin Mary. God was referred to a few times, but our Lord and Saviour Jesus Christ never. Even the private correspondence mentioned above, and from a Christian source, alludes to Him but once, and then indirectly, and by His human and family name, Jesus.

"What place do you give to Christ in Spiritualism?" was asked of a votary by a London editor. "Is He to you the Son of God, and do you worship Him as such?"

"Oh, no," came the reply. "He is to us simply the Master Medium."

In the words of the editor, (The Life of Faith, London), "that confession is fatal. No creed, no cult, no religion that dethrones our Lord and places Him on a level with men and mediums has any right to claim a Christian connection. And men and women who profess to be followers of Christ are putting Him to open shame when they join hands with those who would, if they could, rob Him of His deity and His matchless glory."

SATAN—OR SPIRITISM AT ITS SOURCE

I

Satan is the source of Spiritism, and since the Bible is the only place in which we can learn anything reliable about him, we now open its pages for that purpose.

As we are writing for Christians chiefly, it is assumed that the Bible is the revelation of God and not only credible as to its statements of fact but an inspired record of them. The evidence of this is convincing and never more so than in the twentieth century, as could easily be demonstrated if circumstances permitted or required it.

Even the casual reader of the Bible will recall the outstanding occasions when Satan appears on its scenes. First, as the "serpent" in the Garden of Eden tempting and overcoming our first parents, for twice in the New Testament the serpent is identified with the devil and Satan (Rev. XII. 9; XX. 2). Next, in the history of Job (chapters I and II); then, later, in vision, in the Old Testament as the accuser of Israel after their return from Babylon (Zech. III).

In the New Testament he first comes before us as Christ's tempter in the wilderness (Matthew IV and its parallels); he entered into Judas to betray Christ (John XIII. 27), and into Ananias and Sapphira to lie to the Holy Ghost (Acts V. 3). He hindered Paul in his missionary work (I Thess. II. 18); he is said to walk about as a roaring lion seeking whom he may devour (I Pet. V. 8), and in the end of this age he will give his power to the Lawless one to deceive, if possible, the very elect (Matthew XXIV. 24; 2 Thess. II. 8-10); Rev. XIII. 1, 2).

Satan has many names in Scripture, each of which reveals some feature of his character. "Satan" itself means the Adversary; "devil," (slanderer); "Apollyon," (destroyer); "Beelzebub," (prince of the demons); "Belial," (low, abject); "the wicked one"; "the god of this world"; "the prince of darkness"; "the dragon," "tormentor," "accuser," "deceiver," "liar," "murderer," "he that hath the power of death." This sufficiently reveals the kind of being he is and furnishes a reason why we should beware of him.

II

As to the origin of Satan, those who class the cherubim as angels, think he was one of them, and anointed probably for a position of great authority. This authority may have been over primitive creation, i.e., heaven and earth as at first created, and before the earth became without form and void (Gen. I. 1).

He fell through pride (Isa. XIV. 12-14). Some think he was then cast out of heaven according to Christ's words in Luke X. 18, on which supposition, he then made the earth and the air the scene of his activity (Eph. II. 2; I. Pet. V. 8).

A scriptural basis for this conjecture is in Ezekiel XXVIII. n-15. The chapter is a rebuke of the King of Tyre, but at the verses named the language goes beyond him to Satan described in his unfallen state.

If this interpretation is correct, the chapter teaches much about Satan, which is summed up by Dr. R. A. Torrey in "What the Bible Teaches," thus:

1. He was the sum of created perfection, v. 12.

2. He was in the garden of God, v. 13. This does not mean the Eden of Adam, but an earlier one. The Eden of Adam was remarkable for its vegetable glory, but this for its mineral glory. Cf. Revelation XXI. 10-21.

3. He was the anointed cherub that covereth, v. 14. First, he was a "cherub", the highest rank in the angelic world. Second, "the anointed" cherub, i.e., one who was set apart for a formal work. Third, the anointed cherub that *covereth.* The meaning of this word is not given, though it suggests Exodus XXXVII. 9.

4. He was upon the holy mountain of God, v. 14, which may mean the place where God manifested His personal glory.

5. He walked up and down in the midst of the stones of fire, v. 14. This suggests Exodus XXIV. 10, 17, R.V., and Ezekiel I. 15, 22, 25, 26, R.V. In the former the seventy elders saw the Lord of Israel, and "there was under His feet as it were a paved walk of sapphire stone", and "the appearance of the glory of the Lord was like devouring fire on the top of the mount." This may afford an idea of what the "stones of fire" were, and indicate how near Satan may have been to God.

6. His heart was lifted up because of his beauty, v. 17. Cf. I Timothy III. 6 R.V.

7. He was cast out of the mountain of God, and destroyed from the midst of the stones of fire, v. 16.

8. He shall be cast to the earth and be made a spectacle, vv. 17, 18. Cf. with 2 Thessalonians 11. 8; Revelation XII. 9, 10, and XIX. 20.

III

To go a little further into the nature and character of Satan:

(1) He is a *person*, i.e., he possesses self-consciousness and free-will, because the facts stated in the preceding paragraphs could not be predicted of an influence or a principle of evil.

(2) He has *great dignity*, since he is styled the "prince," "the god of this world," and "prince of the power of the air," and it is said that Michael the Archangel "durst not bring against him a railing judgment," (John XII. 31 52 Cor. IV. 4; Eph. II. 2; Jude 8, 9, R.V.).

(3) He has *great power*, since he is able to control the forces of nature, human property and life, demons, the world-rulers of darkness, and the whole world of men out of Christ, (Job I. 10-12; Luke XL 14-1S; I John V. 19 R.V.; Acts XXVI. 18; Eph. VI. 11, 12).

(4) He has *great cunning and deceit*, since he transforms himself into an angel of light, uses wiles and devices, signs and lying wonders (Matthew XXIV. 24; 2 Cor. II. 11; 2 Cor. XL 14; Eph. VI. 11, 12 R.V.; 2 Thess. II. 9, R.V.)

(5) He has *great malignity*, being called the evil one, a liar, a murderer, and a sinner from the beginning (Matthew V. 37; Luke VIII. 12; John VIII. 44; 2 Cor. IV. 4; I John III. 8).

(6) He has *great fear*, for if we resist him he will flee from us (James IV. 7).

IV

As to Satan's present location and his work, he is referred to as being in the heavenly places, and also as going to and fro in the earth. As in the age to come, Christ and His Church, though abiding in the heavenly places, will rule an earthly people, so now Satan and his hosts abiding in the heavenly places are ruling an earthly people. (Job I. 6, 7; Eph. VI. 11, 12; I Peter V. 8; Rev. XII. 9).

As to his work:

(1) He is the author of sin and tempts to sin (Gen. III. 1-6; I Chron. XXI. 1; Matt. IV);

(2) He produces sickness and has the power of death (Luke XIII. 16; Acts X. 38; Heb. II. 14);

(3) He lays snares for men (I Tim. III. 7);

(4) He takes the Word of God out of their hearts (Matt. XIII. 19);

(5) He puts wicked purposes into their hearts (Eph. IV. 27);

(6) He blinds their minds (2 Cor. IV. 4, R.V.);

(7) He harasses and accuses them (2 Cor. XII. 7; Rev. XIII. 9, 10);

(8) He enters into them (John XIII. 27);

(9) He does all this and more by means of the angelic messengers who carry on his work (2 Cor. XL 14, 15; Rev. III. 9).

Happily however, there are certain limitations of his work and power. For example, being a finite and created being he can be only in one place at one time, though what is done by his agents being attributed to him, he is practically ubiquitous.

In the second place, it is reassuring to know that his influence over the bodies of men is entirely subject to God's control (Job II. 7; Luke XIII. 16; Acts X. 38), and that his influence over the souls of men is simply moral. That is to say, he may offer suggestions and deceive or persuade men, but he is absolutely unable to change their hearts or coerce their wills. "Every man is tempted, when he is drawn away of his own lust, and enticed" (Jas. I. 14).

Our responsibility in regard to Satan therefore, is threefold: We are to watch against him (I Peter V. 8); to give no place to him (Eph. IV. 27); and to resist him (Jas. IV. 7).

We watch against him as the context of the passage shows, by humbling ourselves under the mighty hand of God and casting all our anxiety upon Him. We give no place to him by restraining wrath and eschewing falsehood; and we resist him by the Sword of the Spirit which is the Word of God.

V

It remains to say that there are two ways in which Satan is particularly manifesting himself today in the lives and affairs of men. The Sunday School Times recently called it "the devil's worldwide revival." One is in the form of demonism and the other spiritism, though the two are closely allied.

1. By demonism is meant just now the Worship of demons and human possession by demons. We learn from the Bible that the apostate Israelites sacrificed to demons, and that the gods of the heathen were demons. Paul charged the Athenians with being too much addicted to demon worship, which is the real meaning of the word "superstitious" in Acts XVII. 22. He also adds that the things which the Gentiles sacrificed they sacrificed to demons and not to God.

It is true that the Bible teaching about demoniacal possession has been denied by some, who explain the symptoms referred to as those of physical disease simply. They admit that Christ taught the contrary, but meet this by saying that He conformed His language to the vulgar notions of the times, the same argument as they use with reference to other subjects of His teaching, the Mosaic authorship of the Pentateuch, for example.

Nevertheless, the New Testament puts it beyond question that demoniacs were possessed by demons. For example:

(1) They evinced superhuman strength and knowledge, even recognizing Jesus as the Son of God, as well as His power and purpose to punish the ungodly.

(2) In addressing Him, the demons distinguished themselves from the persons they tormented, saying in the case of the Gadarenes, "What have we to do with Thee, Jesus?" and "If Thou cast us out, suffer us to go away into the deep" (Matt. VIII. 28-31).

(3) In delivering those who were possessed, Christ spoke not to the persons themselves, but to their tormentors, saying to the latter, "Go" or "Come out". In other instances also the demons are expressly distinguished from the diseases they created, as when we read of Christ that they brought unto Him all sick people, *and those that were possessed with demons,* and those that were lunatic.

Nor is demoniacal possession limited to the time of Christ. It existed before Christ came, because the Jews of His day professed to cast out demons, showing that the phenomenon was not new to them; and it existed after He departed, because He commissioned His disciples to cast out demons, a commission upon which they acted.

Early church fathers testify to the casting out of demons in their day, and the Reformation fathers do the same. It exists now as seen in our Missionary annals, especially that recent volume, Demons and Demon Possession, by Dr. Nevius, and in current discussions on Theosophy and Spiritism and Speaking with Tongues.

Finally, demoniacal possession will constitute one of the awful features of the tribulation at the end of this age, as is clearly indicated, in the book of Revelation. The battle of Armageddon for example, is to be brought about by the spirits of demons working miracles (Rev. XVI. 14).

VI

2. The other way in which Satan is manifesting himself and is likely to do so until the end of the age is in Spiritism. The dictionary defines it as the belief that the spirits of the dead communicate with and manifest their presence to men. It is supposed that they usually do this through the agency of a human person called a medium. As was stated before, we deny that the spirits of the dead do this, but we affirm that there is a counterfeit materialization of the dead by demons. That is, demons assume a material and bodily form to deceive the living into the belief that they are communicating with the dead.

In other words, we believe that certain facts of Spiritism are true. There are some things which pass for facts that are not facts, for Satan has no desire that his work should become too apparent, but nevertheless there is a basis of fact underlying the pretensions of Spiritism, which we must not only admit but insist upon as a testimony against it.

The scientists bear witness that while there is a large element of fraud in Spiritism, there is still a residuum of facts demanding explanation. They would refer some of these to the powers of the human mind, the "subliminal consciousness," just below the level of the normal waking life, but there are still other manifestations for which that explanation will not suffice, and to which such men testify as Alfred Russell Wallace, Sir Wm. Crookes, Sir Oliver Lodge and the late

Professor William James of Harvard. It is Sir Wm. Crookes who, in his Evidences of Spiritualism, said "that certain phenomena occur under circumstances in which they can not be explained by any physical law at present known, is a fact of which I am as certain as I am of the most elementary fact in chemistry."

Coming to the Bible however, and it is upon that we stand, v/e find God legislating for Israel, and saying, "A man also, or woman, that hath a familiar spirit, or one that is a wizard, shall surely be put to death (Lev. XX. 27)." This means those who are instructed in the art of intercourse with demons, and the warning it expresses is repeated in one form or another in the Old Testament very frequently as we shall see.

Moreover, take such illustrations as the story of Saul and the Witch of Endor, or that of Paul and the Philippian damsel. The latter was what is now called a medium, and according to the Greek was possessed by the spirit of Pytho, the same that guided the Delphic oracle. Her testimony to Paul and his companions proves that the messengers of Satan sometimes speak truth, when it is to their advantage to do so, but more of this later.

Finally, the Bible asserts the continuance of such Satanic agency throughout this dispensation (Gal. V. 20, 21; Rev. IX. 21; Rev. XVI. 14; Rev. XVIII. 23; and Rev. XXI. 8). Whether it will continue in the form and under the name of Spiritism or not, it is impossible to say, but nevertheless as the end of the age approaches Satan's emissaries will act more and more without disguise, and "show great signs and wonders insomuch that if it were possible they shall deceive the very elect" (Matt. XXIV. 24).

ANGELS AND DEMONS, OR SPIRITISM'S PERSONNEL

I

One can not be very intelligent in Spiritism without knowing something about angels of which the Bible says so much.

The Old Testament or Hebrew word for angel is "Malek", and the New Testament or Greek word, "angellus", both of them meaning "messenger" or "agent". The words are sometimes used of men and even of God Himself, but in the latter case always in the form of "The Angel of the Lord", an expression signifying the presence of the Deity in angelic form. The words are used impersonally in some instances also, but for our present purpose these need not be enumerated.

Angels are spirits, superior to men and inferior to God (Ps. VIII. 4, 5; Heb. I. 7, 8). They would seem to have bodies of some kind (Luke XX. 36), and they have appeared in human form (always as men, not women), and have eaten food and lodged in houses (Gen. XVIII. 8; XIX. 3).

The number of angels is very great (Dan. VII. 10; Ps. LXVIII. 17; Matt. XXVI. 53), and their power likewise, whether exercised in the material or spiritual world (Ps. CIIL 20; 2 Kings XIX. 35; 2 Thess. I. 7). And yet their power and knowledge are both limited (Dan. X. 13; Matt. XXIV. 36; Eph. III. 9, 10).

Angels are employed both in heaven and on earth. In heaven they are worshippers (Matt. XVIII. 10; Rev. V. 11), but on earth they are associated with the affairs of providence, doing good to God's people and executing judgment on God's enemies, the latter ministry to be intensified at the end of the age (Ps. XC. 10-12; 2 Kings XIX. 35; I Thess. IV. 17).

There appear to be graded positions and authority among them judging by the allusions to thrones, dominions, principalities and powers (Eph. I. 21), and by the mention of Michael as the Archangel (Dan. X. 13), and Gabriel as one who stands "in the presence of God" (Luke I. 19).

There is a tendency towards speculation in considering these beings against which we are earnestly warned in Paul's letter to the Colossians; speculation that in the case of the Roman Catholic Church especially leads to superstition and their voluntary worship. On the other hand however, Protestantism may have thought too little about them, and have thereby greatly impoverished her experience of Divine providence and her sense of succor and comfort in times of peril and sorrow, that succor and comfort which it is their office under God to freely and graciously supply.

II

But up until this point we have been dealing entirely with good or holy angels, while alas ! there is another class of them, evil as well as good.

And the evil angels are again divided into two classes. One consists of those that are in chains of darkness reserved unto judgment (2 Peter II. 4) and the other of those that are actively engaged in evil, with Satan at their head. The latter are those of which Paul speaks in Eph. VI. 11, 12, where believers are exhorted to "put on the whole armor of God" that they "may be able to stand against the wiles of the devil," because they wrestle "against principalities, against powers, against the world-rulers of this darkness, and spiritual hosts of wickedness in the heavenly places." (See also Matthew XXV. 41; Rev. XII. 9).

It is these that are in evidence, it is believed, in the present "spiritist invasion." Of their origin we know nothing more than we do of the good angels, which is simply that they were created by God (Col. I. 16).

It is assumed also that all were created good, but that some fell as did Satan himself, though just when, or why they fell, God is not pleased to reveal. The following named Scriptures tell us about all we can know of the matter, John VIII. 44; I Tim. III. 6, 7; 2 Peter II. 4; Jude 6, 7. From these we surmise that they abode not in the knowledge and worship of God, but fell into condemnation through pride. They kept not their first estate or principality, so to speak, but left their proper habitation.

They are described sometimes as evil spirits (Judges IX. 23; Luke VII. 21), unclean spirits Matt. X. 1), and demons (Deut. XXXII. 17; Matt. VII. 22). This last word is erroneously rendered "devils" in the King James Version, as there is but one devil, who is identical with Satan, but there are many demons. So many indeed as to compose a kingdom with a leader, or prince (Luke VIII. 30; Matt. XII. 24-26; Eph. VI. 12).

These demons are called Satan's agents in Matt. XII. 26, 27 and XXV. 41, and as such they seem able to inflict physical maladies on men (Matt. XII. 22; XVII. 15-18; Luke XIII. 16; and even enter and control their bodies and those of beasts also (Mark V. 13; Acts XVI. 16); while from the moral point of view they are able to seduce men from the truth and lead them into all uncleanness (I Kings XXII. 22; I Tim. IV. 1; 2 Peter II. 10-12).

It is especially important to note that these demons maintain a conflict with Christian believers (Eph. VI. 12), and that God Himself sometimes uses them in judgment upon unbelievers and wicked men (Judges IX. 23; I Sam. XVI. 14). They are to be used in the awful judgments upon the earth in the Tribulation period (Rev. IX. 1-11; XVI. 13, 14); but their own eternal fate, like that of their mighty but unholy leader, is one of torment (Matt. VIII. 29; Luke VIII. 31).

A deeply interesting question, and a very practical one also, is that of the present abode of these evil spirits or demons. Keep in mind in the reply that there are two classes of them, the one reserved in chains of darkness of which we shall learn more by and by, and whose abode is hell or "Tartarus" (Greek); and the other occupying the air considered as one of the "heavenly places" so frequently mentioned in the New Testament. From this place however, they will be cast down to earth prior to the Millenium, and then at length go into the lake of fire and brimstone "prepared for the devil and his angels" (Rev. XII. 7-9; Matt. XXV. 41).

III

In the preceding chapter we discussed the topic of demon worship and demon possession sufficiently for our present purpose, and only allude to it again as leading up to an earnest warning and appeal.

Remember that which was previously stated. (1), that demon possession is distinct from physical disease; (2), that it was and is not limited to the time of Christ; and (3) that it is in evidence today and is predicted as one of the awful features of the Tribulation at the end of this age.

Quoting from the Rev. F. B. Meyer, D.D., of London, in his booklet just from the press:

"They hate to be unclothed, and would rather inhabit swine than have no covering (Matt. VIII. 31). The nakedness of an evil spirit is torment before the time (Matt. VIII. 29; Mark V. 7).

"Their one object is to reduce the human race and drag it to their own degraded condition. Just as the Divine Spirit can only achieve His end by and through our instrumentality —and therefore, we are called to present our bodies to Him—so the great adversary can only achieve his end by and through human instruments, and therefore steals gradually over the consciousness of his victims until they are taken captive by the devil at his will (2 Tim. II. 26).

"Apparently the Almighty has locked and bolted our human nature against the intrusion of the demon-world, and it is at our peril that we open the door from within or allow it to be broken in from without. The angels will not attempt to help us unless at the express command of the Almighty; but demon-spirits are disobedient and recalcitrant. They defy the Divine prohibition; and if they fail to break in by force, they can at least induce the human soul to connive at their entrance by opening the door from within; and when the door has been opened once it can be opened repeatedly, and each time more easily, until the power of resistance is gone, and the demon can go and come at will, or introduce seven companions worse than himself.

"A man of high repute told me recently that a lady had come to him complaining that her life was made a perfect torment by the suggestion of unclean spirits, of which she could not rid herself. She had been an habitue of séances, and now was held by a kind of obsession. He entreated her to promise to tear herself from their fatal spell, and she promised to go to but one more, on the following day. But that day she became raving mad, rushed in an almost nude condition into the public thoroughfare, and has been for the last two years in an asylum.

"If there has been any tampering with the demon-world, the urgency for immediate arrest is imperative, lest the current become too swift to be arrested by the oarsman, though he pull against it with the agony of despair." —The Modern Craze of Spiritualism, pp. 10, 11.

SPIRITISM BEFORE THE FLOOD

I

The task we have set ourselves would be inadequately rendered if attention were not called to the mysterious sixth chapter of Genesis, whose record of the marriages of "the sons of God" with "the daughters of men" and the issue of the same is intended to account for the catastrophe of the flood. The text follows:

> "And it came to pass, when men began to multiply on the face of the earth, and daughters were born unto them,
>
> "That the sons of God saw the daughters of men that they were fair; and they took them wives of all which they chose.
>
> "And the Lord said, My spirit shall not always strive with man, for that he also is flesh: yet his days shall be an hundred and twenty years.
>
> "There were giants in the earth in those days; and also after that, when the sons of God came in unto the daughters of men, and they bare children to them, the same became mighty men which were of old, men of renown."

The question arises, Who were these "sons of God" and these "daughters of men" whose union produced the powerful and wicked race the iniquity of which resulted thus and necessitated this judgment?

We who are familiar with the use of the first-named phrase in the New Testament might at first interpret it to mean men of faith, true believers, godly saints; while the second would logically apply to women of the opposite character.

But reflection would recall that Moses was unlikely to be using New Testament terms, and that such phraseology would be foreign to conditions ante-dating the flood.

Also, it might be asked, would godly men contract such marriages and in such a way, inasmuch as a plurality of wives and force in obtaining them seem to be implied? And even if they did, what would further explain the gigantic stature and colossal wickedness of their offspring bringing about so terrible a penalty as the flood?

In searching for a different explanation we find that "sons of God" is used everywhere else in the Old Testament to designate angels, and why should it not be so used here? Moreover if it were so used, it would carry with it a confounding of two distinct orders of creatures and the production of a mixed race, partly human, partly super-human, which would be just such a derangement of the Divine plan as to warrant that which occurred, namely, the almost total extermination of all who were upon the earth.

Indeed this was the prevailing view of the passage in the ancient synagogue of the Jews and among Christian theologians for the first three or four centuries of the Church. And there is reason to believe it would not have changed in the latter case, had it not been for certain erroneous opinions and practices of Christendom, to which reference will be made later, and with which it was not in harmony.

But naturally there exists a prejudice against such a view. How could such intercourse be possible between the visible and invisible worlds, such an unnatural connection between beings so widely different from each other?

It is our purpose to deal with this question before we conclude, but a more important one precedes it. It is not, as Nicodemus said, "How *can* these things be?" but rather, Is it true that they *are*? However inconceivable or inexplicable the fact may be, it is first necessary to show that it is a fact.

In doing this we now address ourselves to two theories that have been most persistently maintained in opposition to it. The first, a Jewish interpretation which holds the "sons of God" to mean men of authority or rank who married women of inferior station; and the second, the Church interpretation already mentioned, which holds that godly men, the descendants of Seth for example, chose for wives women of godless life belonging to the line of Cain.

II

The Jewish interpretation has been paraphrased thus: "When men began to multiply on the earth the chief men took wives of all the handsome poor women they chose. They were tyrants in the earth of those days. Also, after the antediluvian days, powerful men had unlawful connexions with the inferior women, and the children which sprang from this illicit intercourse were the renowned heroes of antiquity, of whom the heathen made their gods."

The ground on which this interpretation was founded is that the Hebrew word for God, *Elohim*, is sometimes used in the Old Testament to denote judges or princes, hence "sons of God" might mean sons of judges or sons of princes. And the Hebrew word for man, *Adam*, is occasionally used to denote one whose station in the world is lowly or poor, hence "daughters of men" might mean daughters of the lowly or the poor.

It is admitted that *Elohim* (gods) is, in a few instances, applied in the Old Testament to Israelitish magistrates acting representatively for Jehovah, but there is nothing in this passage of that character. Moreover this word is not *Elohim* simply, but *Bne-ha-Elohim*, a very different expression, which means "sons of God", and which in every other instance stands, not for men of any grade or distinction, but for angels. Therefore, the inference is fair that if in this place, Moses had intended men however great, he would not have used that word but some other, of which there were several from which to choose.

It is admitted also that *Adam* is, in some places, applied to human beings of low degree, but when women of low degree are meant the word is always used in connection with the word *Ish*, which is not the case here. Otherwise the word simply means a man, or mankind in general, without distinction of class or condition. Moreover the particular word now under discussion is not *Adam* simply, but *Bnoth-ha-Adam*, "daughters of Men," which occurs nowhere else in the Old Testament, so that no argument can be founded upon its usage.

"In short," to quote another, "women of high station as well as low are *Bnoth-ha-Adam*," and the title simply means Adam's daughters, female descendants, womankind without distinction.

Indeed it is difficult to understand how such an interpretation of the passage ever found acceptance considering its extreme improbability. How unlikely, to continue quoting, "that all the great men of the day, or even a large proportion of them, should, at the same time and with one consent, contract such alliances? And how unlikely that female beauty should just then have appeared, and only or chiefly, in women of the lower rank; and that it should have possessed such strongly attractive power in the case of all these "sons of God"?

And stranger still, how improbable the results that followed? Why should it have come about that the marriage of the judges, or princes, of that age with women of low degree but of great beauty, should have issued in mighty men of renown, a heroic race of gigantic size, celebrated for their exploits through succeeding time?

And strangest of all, the Hebrew word for "giants" in verse four is *Nephilim*, which means "fallen ones," as to whom there can be little doubt that they were more than human beings and derived their origin in part from a superhuman source.

A word of explanation seems necessary before leaving the Jewish interpretation, by which of course is not meant that of the ancient Jewish synagogue mentioned above, but that of Jewish teachers of a later time, say, the early centuries of the Christian era. The Jewish synagogue, as was said, held to the angel interpretation.

Just what prompted the change of interpretation from that of angels to that of great men is not known except that it could not have been on exegetical grounds. Fleming, from whose work on The Fallen Angels and the Heroes of Mythology we are quoting, thinks it may have been dogmatic considerations concerning the nature of angels of which we shall speak by and by; but suffice for the present to re-affirm that the angelic interpretation was the first which suggested itself, and that it was very anciently received both by Jews and Christians.

III

A fair and clear statement of the later Christian, or Church, interpretation is given by Dr. John Gill in his Exposition of the Old Testament, published in the middle of the 18th century. He says: "Those sons of God were not angels, because angels are incorporeal beings, and can not be affected with fleshly lusts, or marry and be given in marriage, or generate and be generated. Nor were they the sons of judges, magistrates and great personages; but rather is the phrase to be understood of the posterity of Seth, who from the time of Enos, when men began to be called by the Name of the Lord (Gen. IV. 26), had the title of 'sons of God' in distinction from the children of men."

All this is pure assumption on Dr. Gill's part, and was to be expected, since no serious attempt seems to have been made by him to ascertain the real meaning of the words in their place whatever the consequences might be. For example, what ground outside of his own opinion, had he for saying that angels are incorporeal, etc.? And similarly, what ground for saying all that he does say about the posterity of Seth?

However, he has plenty of company among commentators and others, including some of the poets, Milton as an illustration, in Paradise Lost. And yet, that great poet, in Paradise Regained Book II, returns to the angel interpretation, where he makes Satan, after the failure of his first temptation of Christ, in addressing the infernal council, say to Belial:

> "Before the flood, thou with thy lusty crew,
> False titled sons of God, roaming the earth,
> Cast wanton eyes on the daughters of men,
> And coupled with them, and begot a race."

What, however, explains the abandonment of the earlier angel interpretation for this of the sons of Seth? The most likely answer is that of John Henry Kurtz, D.D., professor of theology at Dorpat, quoted at some length by Fleming, who attributes it to the rise of certain superstitions and unwarrantable practices in the church growing out of false ideas as to the nature of angels.

In other words, it was the coming in of angel worship that drove it out. Angel worship raised its head gradually, but its progress tended to remove everything that might shake confidence in the holiness of angels, or mar the gratification which their worship afforded.

There was also a second cause which was almost equally influential with the first, namely the spread of celibacy, or monkery, as Kurtz calls it, and the reverence with which it came to be regarded in the early centuries. If Genesis VI. 1-4 taught that although the angels in heaven marry not, yet at one time a portion of them, seduced by the beauty of women, came down to earth for the purpose of gratifying amorous propensities, then a weakness of the like kind on the part of "earthly angels" might be more readily excused. As a matter of fact such an apology was pleaded for monkish transgressions, at the time, and it therefore became a pretext for changing angelic "sons of God" into human "sons of God."

It was not until the last century that the angel interpretation began again to find favor with Christian theologians. And for its revival by the way, we are, in a sense, indebted to the destructive critics. Their attacks upon the Bible necessitated a return to the old-fashioned way of studying it with the aid of the grammar and lexicon. Exegesis thus has been restored to its rightful place, and exegesis never attempts to explain away uncommon or supernatural occurrences just because it does not understand them.

We have spoken of Fleming's work on The Fallen Angels, but he, in turn, is indebted to Kurtz above named, and to Maitland's essays on the same subject and on False Worship, as well as to Kitto's Daily Bible Illustrations. Following these authorities he goes on to deal at length with collateral aspects of the question for which we have not the space or time except to mention them. They include the suppositions and assumptions that are involved in the Sethite interpretation, an examination of Genesis IV. 26, which speaks of Seth's descendants, a careful inquiry into the use of a phrase analogous to "the sons of God" wherever it occurs either in the Old or New Testament, and the antithesis of the "sons of God" and "daughters of men."

We have studied him with care, and feel convinced that the improbabilities involved in the Sethite, or as we have called it, the Church interpretation, are so serious as to put it out of court.

IV

In the next chapter we deal with the angel interpretation and the objections to it growing out of the supposed nature of angels. But we conclude this with some general observations in anticipation of it:

1. It has already been suggested that while angels are immaterial beings, yet they appear to possess, or at least are able to assume, some kind of an ethereal, corporeal form. At the same time it is to be remembered that the human race is composed of immaterial beings,

clothed at present with gross bodies akin to beasts, but hereafter, in the case of the redeemed at least, to be clothed with spiritual bodies not unlike that of angels. If, therefore, there is in our nature a capability of becoming like angels in some degree, is it so certain that they are as dissimilar to us in all respects as many people believe?

2. We have seen also that angels, both good and bad, are interested in the affairs of men, and have communicated with men. How much more intimate that communication might have been had not sin entered the human family, who can say? And if there is a possibility of greater communication if God willed it so, is it unlikely that evil angels, should it suit their propensities, would endeavor to make it so whether it was His will or not?

"We can not hold it to be an absurd proposition," writes Kurtz, quoted by Fleming, "that angels who, in their state of holiness, desire to look into the deepest mystery of grace on earth (I Peter I. 12), should, in their apostasy from holiness, have desired to look into the deepest mystery of nature on earth; and, transgressing the limits of their own nature, participate in that mystery themselves."

"SONS OF GOD" MARRYING THE "DAUGHTERS OF MEN"

I

In the preceding chapter we have seen that Spiritism in one of its forms was directly responsible for the flood. The "sons of God" who took to themselves wives of "the daughters of men" (Genesis VI), were evil angels, who entered upon that intercourse the offspring of which were the "Nephilim," "the fallen ones," the mighty heroes of antiquity. These in their turn, presumably, furnished the ground for the stories of the loves of the gods and demigods of classic lore.

The proof of this being presented, as well as its corroboration by the ancient Jewish synagogue and the early Christian writers, it remains to more fully consider objections raised against it on the ground of the nature of angels as well as the teaching of our Lord in Matthew XXII. 30.

It is said for example, that an angel is altogether spiritual and immaterial, and hence such implied intercourse is impossible.

To this it might only be necessary to reply,

(1) Even if it were true, even if the angelic nature were such, it could not change the fact stated in the text, that "the sons of God" took to themselves wives of "the daughters of men," the offspring of which were as described. Nor could it change the fact that "sons of God" is a phrase everywhere in the Old Testament used of angels, and not men.

That is to say, faith does not wait to learn the possibility of a thing before it believes it. It believes it on the evidence presented, assuming its possibility until the opposite has been shown.

In this case, however, "impossibility never can be shown until an exhaustive knowledge is possessed of all that is possible to angels in the line of sinful degeneracy within the powers bestowed upon them at creation." (Kurtz, quoted by Fleming, p. 89.)

(2) This leads to the remark that no one is qualified to say just what the angelic nature may be, because no one really knows. On the other hand, the implications are against the spiritual and immaterial idea as shown in our former chapters dealing with satan, angels and demons. Angels have appeared to men in human form, and have been taken for men, and have partaken of food like human beings.

It may be said that these were instances where God wrought miracles to produce the phenomenon, and hence that they furnish no standard for judging of what angels in rebellion might do.

But what right have we to suppose a miracle? The Bible being silent on the question of a miracle in such instances, why should we introduce it? Especially, why should we do so when we know that the working of miracles on God's part is reserved for great emergencies?

Moreover, angels themselves may work miracles, as we have already seen. What about Satan's assumption of the body of a serpent in Eden? What about the magicians withstanding Moses in Egypt? What about the beast with the two horns in the book of Revelation (XIII, 11-15), and "the spirits of demons working miracles which go forth unto the kings of the whole world to gather them to the battle of that great day of God Almighty?" (Rev. XVI, 13, 14.)

Angels do not possess power to create something out of nothing, which is alone the prerogative of God, but they may be able so to combine existing elements as to form for themselves bodies similar to the human.

(3) It may be questioned whether there is any being in the universe who is simply spiritual and immaterial, except the Infinite Himself, Who is above and beyond all time and space. Isaac Taylor in his Physical Theory of Another Life, takes the position that the idea of an absolutely incorporeal being is irreconcilable with that of a finite creature, because anything created can subsist and work only within the limits of time and space, and corporeality confines the creature to such limits. It is God only Who exists above and beyond these limits.

In other words, an embodied state of some kind is indispensable to a finite mind, whose faculties can not otherwise come into play or produce effects.

(4) As Fleming reminds us, should all these views still be unsatisfactory, there remains the fact that human bodies have been possessed by evil spirits, which may have been the case here. Through the medium of such bodies thus possessed, "the sons of God" may have had the intercourse referred to.

Indeed this has been the opinion of some of the older commentators, and is suggested as early as the Clementine Homilies (Hom. IX). It is a very simple, and yet sufficient, solution of the difficulty, for we are taught in the Gospels that the powers and faculties of the human being thus possessed were completely controlled, intensified and directed by the demon, or else that the two natures, in some incomprehensible manner were interfused and the weaker overborne by the stronger.

The remarkable physical proportions, the superhuman strength and the evil disposition of the Nephilim would be the natural effects of such a power imparted to human beings by fallen spirits. Nor would such possession necessarily involve the suffering of physical and mental evils to which demoniacs of the Gospels were subjected, for Satan can transform himself into an angel of light, and no doubt his emissaries would conduct themselves in a way to accomplish the object they had in view. (The Fallen Angels, p. 95.)

(5) One more supposition is still to be considered, namely, that "the sons of God" in their spiritual nature, or at the most in some kind of subtle, ethereal body, or with the appearance of a human body, might in some incomprehensible way effect what the text in Genesis declares to have been the fact. Augustine in the City of God, book 15, thinks this possible; and so also does Dr. Henry More, an English divine and philosopher of the seventeenth century (Mystery of Godliness, book III, C. 18), and the Rev. Theo. Campbell in the Irish Ecclesiastical Gazette, 1867, all quoted by Fleming.

Of course this involves difficulties of its own, and is not presented as a solution, but merely as a supposition worthy of consideration. Those who wish to consider it further will find a good deal of information in a book easily accessible, known as Earth's Earliest Ages, by G. H. Pember, pp. 205-213, 375-391, edition of 1885, Armstrong, New York.

We quote a paragraph or two from this work:

"Spiritualists teach that all will marry in the next world, if they do not in this; and that true marriage lasts through eternity. The natural inference is that the true spouses of some are already in the spirit-land. And to such an extent is this inference followed out that many are reported to be receiving visits and communications from those spiritual beings with whom they are to be united forever. The ceremonious marriage of a woman to a demon is a thing not unknown in the United States."

He mentions a book called "An Angel's Message," claiming to be communications from a spirit to an English lady, his destined bride for eternity. The demon-lover describes himself as the spirit of a man of deep religious feeling, who, during his sojourn in the flesh was accustomed to visit the house of the lady's father, though at that time he found no attraction in her. In the course of years he died, as did also the mother of the lady. Soon after the decease of the latter her daughter began to receive communications understood to come from the mother, in the course of which the demon-lover is introduced, and thereafter inspires the medium, (i.e., the lady in the case) himself. It is she who, under his inspiration and control now pens the following:

"She who writes these lines is my wife more than may be thought possible by those who have not had a similar state opened in themselves. She is not so as to her natural body, but she is so as to her spiritual body. For 'there is a natural body, and there is a spiritual body.' The one is within the other as a kernel within a shell.

"But this state can come to the outward perception of those only who are open to spirit-intercourse. No others can perceive, during their life in the world of nature, that which belongs to the spirit alone. This state constitutes mediumship; for she who is mine is not only a writing medium, but she is also susceptible of very palpable impressions of my presence with her. We are one; and she has received the assurance of that truth by other means than the merely being told so in these writings."

There is much more to the same effect; but that which we have quoted is sufficient to unveil the danger which may be threatening many.

II

It remains to speak of our Lord's words in Matthew XXII, 30, and the parallels, where in rebuking the Sadducees, He says:

> "Ye do err, not knowing the Scriptures nor the power of God.
> For in the resurrection they neither marry nor are given in marriage, but are the angels of God in heaven."

Two ways of meeting this objection in harmony with the foregoing have been suggested. One is, to say that Christ is speaking of the holy angels only, from which no inference is to be drawn as to that of which the same beings might be capable if fallen from their original state.

The other is, that He is stressing the word "heaven", meaning that they do not marry in heaven, but saying nothing as to what they might do under other circumstances or in a different environment. The first is the view of Kurtz the theologian, and the second that of Nagelsbach, the commentator, in the Lange series.

But is either hypothesis a necessity? It is true that angels always appear in the Bible as masculine, never feminine, the former being the gender used of beings in whom "sexual distinctions do not exist; but is it inconceivable that the germ of such distinction may be latent in their nature?"

Man, for example, was not created to sin, and yet he had in his constitution the capability of sinning, a capability which came into operation in his departing from the ordinance of the Creator. In like manner it is thought, the germ spoken of as a possibility in the angelic nature might be unfolded as a result of wilful departure from the original condition of existence, and the sinking to a lower and unnatural state in apostasy from God.

Our author quotes Paradise Lost, Book I, where Milton names the chiefs of the fallen angels after the idols of the Canaanites and others, and of some he says, they bore the names

> "Of Baalim and Ashtaroth, those male,
> These feminine, for spirits, when they please,
> Can either sex assume, or both; so soft
> And uncompounded is their essence pure."

Finally, following Kurtz again, there is an analogy seen in the resurrection life of man. In this world he has the distinction of sex, but in that which is beyond, i.e., in heaven, he will neither marry nor be given in marriage, but in that respect be equal to the angels.

"Therefore, is it unlawful to infer that, in the event of the angels falling, by their own wilful act, from the higher to the lower sphere of existence, a degradation of their nature, analogous to the elevation in the other case, may take place, and that thus might be developed that power which belonged to the lower grade, but of which the principle always existed in the upper?"

ABOMINATIONS OF THE CANAANITES

I

In introducing the theme of this chapter we return for the moment to Genesis VI, 4, which was under consideration in the two immediately preceding. That verse read,

> "There were giants in the earth in those days; and also after that, when the sons of God came in unto the daughters of men, and they bare children to them, the same became mighty men which were of old, men of renown."

We have seen that "giants" is in the Hebrew, "Nephilim," which means the "fallen ones," or the "fallen angels" identifying them, as we think correctly, with the "sons of God." Others indeed would identify them with the "mighty men," the "men of renown" also mentioned in the verse as the offspring of the marriages of the "sons of God" with the "daughters of men." But for our present purpose it is not essential which application is made as we are chiefly interested in the phrase, "and also, after that."

Some would limit this phrase to the antediluvian age, and interpret it as meaning that after the first irruption of the fallen angels and the warning of God concerning it, others also occurred with like results during the 120 years of respite, until it repented the Lord that He had made man on the earth and He determined to destroy him.

Others, however, would say that it had a postdiluvian application, and that the word and the fact for which it stands come to light again in the history of the Canaanities whom Israel dispossessed, as illustrated in Numbers XIII, 33. At that chapter and verse some of the spies whom Moses dispatched to bring a report of the land returned with the story that all the people were men of great stature; "and there we saw the giants (Nephilim) the sons of Anak, which come of the giants (Nephilim); and we were in our own sight as grasshoppers, and so we were in their sight."

In this instance the same word seems to be used for the "fallen ones" and their offspring both of which were "giants" or "nephilim"; and the circumstance of their presence in that land seems to account for God's command to extirpate the Canaanites much as the greater judgment had fallen upon the whole race at the flood.

II

The above, however, is merely introductory to a consideration of the general teaching of the Old Testament on the subject of Spiritism and its related phenomena following the flood.

To quote the author of The Vital Choice: Endor or Calvary, "the existence of mediums—individuals who, having discovered that they had certain gifts, made a practice of communicating with the spirit world—is taken for granted in the Bible, where they are referred to as wizards, witches, necromancers, etc. The details of their methods are not given to any extent, but what we do know about them leads us to suppose that, with the possible exception of automatic writing, there is no material difference in their methods from those now in vogue."

Indeed, even this exception may be unnecessary. For example, a certain class of the magicians both in Egypt and Babylon were known as "sacred scribes" (Genesis XLI, 8, margin), the root Hebrew word meaning a "style" or pen, and signifying those members of the priestly caste whose magic was somewhat concerned with writing.

Pember thinks they may have been identical with the writing mediums of our day, whom he speaks of as divided into five classes:

(1) Those whose passive hand is moved by the spirit without any mental volition of their own;

(2) Those into whose mind each word is separately insinuated at the moment of its inscription;

(3) Those who write from the dictation of spirit-voices;

(4) Those who copy words and sentences projected before them in letters of light; and

(5) Those in whose presence spirit-hands, visible, or invisible, take up the pen and write the words.

Of course the attitude of the Bible, or rather the attitude of God, for the Bible is the revelation of His mind and will, is that of absolute and unsparing condemnation of all these things, not only because the glory of His Name is involved, but also the highest and eternal welfare of the race which He has created and redeemed.

A few illustrations of this attitude are given:

Take for example, the command at Sinai, "Thou shalt not suffer a witch to live" (Exodus XXII. 18). This can not be concerned with mere superstition or deception, there must be reality behind it, real and wilful fellowship with the powers of evil, or such a penalty would not follow.

And this suggestion is strengthened by the repetition of the command in Leviticus (XX. 27) "A man also, or a woman, that hath a familiar spirit, or that is a wizard, shall surely be put to death; they shall stone them with stones; their blood shall be upon them."

The Hebrew word for "familiar spirit" is pronounced "ob" or "ohv", and means the same as "necromancer", one who professes to talk with the dead or with Satan. This shows conclusively that the inhabitation of any one with an "ohv" must have been the result of voluntary acquiescence, since God would not thus punish that which was involuntary.

"Wizard" is a different word, but its significance is not essentially dissimilar, viz., a knowing person, one instructed in the art of holding intercourse with demons.

It may be of interest to explain that the word "ohv" originally signified a skin bottle, i.e., a skin filled with wine, and hence inflated and tumid. This tumidity being a characteristic of those in whom a demon or an "ohv" dwelt, the word came to be applied both to the person thus affected and to the spirit that caused it. Parkhurst, in his Hebrew and Chaldee Lexicon, quotes a passage in Virgil which describes the swollen and altered form of the Pythoness or demon-possessed woman, and adds, "this shows what the heathen meant in speaking of their diviners being *pleni deo*, full of the god."

III

We now come to the remarkable passage in the eighteenth of Deuteronomy which gives the title to this chapter. It is part of Moses' farewell to Israel before his departure out of this life, and just prior to their entrance upon Canaan, under Joshua:

> "When thou art come into the land which the Lord thy God giveth thee, thou shalt not learn to do after the abominations of those nations. There shall not be found among you any one that maketh his son or his daughter to pass through the fire, or that useth divination, or an observer of times, or an enchanter, or a witch. Or charmer, or a consulter with familiar spirits or a wizard, or a necromancer."

I. Let us study the meaning of these terms:

Passing "through the fire" has been taken by some to mean the worship of Moloch referred to in Leviticus XVIII. 21. Moloch was a god of the Phenicians, whose worship embraced human sacrifice of the most terrible nature, for example, the passing of live infants through the folded arms of the image heated to a white heat.

But that application in the present case is now considered incorrect, and it is thought that the words really mean "a sort of purification by fire, or, a fire baptism, by which the worshippers were consecrated to the god, and supposed to be freed from the fear of a violent death." It was a kind of charm or spell, and hence classed here with sorcery or witchcraft.

Occasion has been taken in the earlier chapters to warn readers against playing with the semblance of these wicked things because of their subtle and alluring power, and another occasion offers itself at this point. It is suggested in a footnote of Pember's, Earth's Earliest Ages (p. 258), where he affirms that this practice is still kept up in parts of Christendom by the midsummer fires of St. John's eve. He quotes a Wesleyan minister as saying that, at Midsummer, on many of the hills of Herefordshire, England, fires were burning, while the peasantry danced around them; and the ceremony was not completed until some of the young people had passed "through the fire."

A second command is against using "divination", which the Revised Version renders "practising augury." This, however, does not clear up the meaning of the word very much, since "augury" is defined as the art of foretelling by signs or omens, a species of modern fortune-telling in which alas! not a few professing Christians are guilty of indulging.

"An observer of times." The English rendering of this would indicate a diviner by the clouds, but the Hebrew simply suggests such observation as requires the use of the eye in minute inspection, and might apply to the entrails of victims. Pember however finds in it the meaning of a fascinator with the eyes, or in modern language, a mesmerist, one who throws another into a magnetic sleep and obtains oracular sayings from him.

"Enchanter" is not regarded as an accurate translation of the Hebrew, which simply seems to denote quick observation of some kind, either of the eye or ear, and then of divining. The observation may be that of the singing or the flight of birds or other aerial phenomena.

"Witch" or "wizard" is translated elsewhere "sorcerer", and means "to pray", but its application shows that the prayer is directed to false gods or demons.

"Charmer", "consulter with familiar spirits", "wizard", "necromancer", are the words used in verse 11, on which Benjamin Wills Newton, another English author, remarks: "Comparing verse 11 with verse 10, the last-named treats of those kinds of divination in which demons are not immediately addressed, but consulted by the intervention of signs or enchantments, while verse 11 implies a more direct appeal to evil spirits."

Thus the first word "charmer", literally means to bind or join together, and applies to one who by incantations and invocations seeks to bring demons into association with himself. Some séances are opened with the chanting or singing of hymns for this object, which leads Mr. Newton to say, very properly, "let no one who sings hymns in spiritualistic séances and thus invokes demons ever dare to sing unto God, for he is not a worshipper of God, but of Satan."

The remainder of the words in this verse so approximate the others in meaning as to make it unnecessary to enlarge upon them.

IV

II. Let us give attention to the command and the warning that follow the terms used:

> "For all that do these things are an abomination unto the Lord: and because of these abominations the Lord thy God doth drive them out from before thee.
> "Thou shall be perfect with the Lord thy God.
> "For these nations, which thou shalt possess, hearkened unto observers of times, and unto diviners; but as for thee, the Lord thy God hath not suffered thee so to do."

An "abomination" is that which God detests, and which He must cast away or separate from Himself. Just what this meant in the mundane sphere, to the nation of the Canaanites, is revealed in the book of Joshua. But what it meant to them as individuals in the life to come, if unrepentant, who can appreciate or describe?

But if these things were an abomination in God's sight then, must they not be an abomination still? Has there been any change in His nature or in their nature? If He detested and cast them away from Himself then, must He not detest and cast them away from Himself now?

In other words, how can the Spiritist, and his kind, expect God's favor either in this world or that which is to come? Insanity multiplying as one of the results of this unholy intercourse is only symptomatic after all. A casting away from God goes deeper and farther than that.

"Thou shalt be perfect with the Lord thy God." "Perfect" in the margin reads, "upright or sincere." God is addressing only His chosen people, those whom He had redeemed from Egypt, and who, amid the thunders and lightnings of Sinai had avowed, "All that the Lord hath spoken we will do" (Exodus XIX. 8).

To be "upright or sincere" meant that they should keep that vow, and to keep it was incompatible with the worship and service of demons. Worship and service is something more than a ceremonial or a prayer. It implies trust, submission, obedience. They who seek unto wizards, and necromancers and diviners, do so for counsel and advice, and for information concerning the unknown which influences both character and conduct. In other words, it begets trust and confidence in, and commands submission and obedience to the false gods represented by those unhappy beings.

No wonder it should be written, "As for thee, the Lord thy God hath not suffered thee so to do." Israel might so do, but they must suffer for it. If not in all respects as the Canaanites suffered who were not His chosen, yet so as to lead them to "see it to be an evil thing and a bitter that thou hast forsaken the Lord thy God" (Jeremiah II. 19).

V

III. The command and the warning is followed by a promise:

"The Lord thy God will raise up unto thee a Prophet from the midst of thee, of thy brethren, like unto me; unto him ye shall hearken;

"According to all that thou desiredst of the Lord thy God in Horeb in the day of the assembly, saying, Let me not hear again the voice of the Lord my God, neither let me see this great fire any more, that I die not.

"And the Lord said unto me, They have well spoken that which they have spoken. I will raise them up a Prophet from among their brethren, like unto thee, and will put my words in his mouth; and he shall speak unto them all that I shall command him.

"And it shall come to pass, that whosoever will not hearken unto my words which he shall speak in my name, I will require it of him."

When the law was given Israel at Horeb, by an audible voice, so terrible was the sight that even Moses said, "I exceedingly fear and quake," and the people "entreated that the word should not be spoken to them anymore" (Heb. XII. 19). "Go thou near," said they to Moses, "and hear all that the Lord our God shall say; and speak thou unto us all that the Lord our God shall speak unto thee; and we will hear it, and do it" (Deuteronomy V. 27).

God took them at their word, and graciously appointed Moses to be their mediator. And now that he was about to be taken from them ere they crossed the Jordan, a successor had already been announced. Joshua was the prophet from the midst of them like unto Moses whom God had raised up, and unto whom they were to hearken.

They need not fear to follow Joshua just as they had followed Moses, and the secret of their continued blessing, victory and prosperity depended on their obeying the one as they had the other. Whoso would not hearken unto Joshua's words as unto Moses, words which would be put "in his mouth" by God, and which he would speak in His Name, it would be required of him.

Manifestly, Joshua was but the type of all the other prophets and commanders of the people who should follow him, and whom God sent to Israel in the later days, "rising up early and sending them," as is so often repeated in the language of Jeremiah, and to whom alas! they would not listen.

But very especially is Joshua the type of Christ as the New Testament so definitely declares (John I. 17; Acts III. 19-26). And it is this last-mentioned fact that brings the command and the warning, as well as the promise, up to date. Here God brings us face to face with His Son in whose mouth His words are, and concerning whom it comes to us with cumulative force that God will require it of any one who fails to listen to and obey what He says.

But it must not be supposed that Christ's words are limited to the few He spake while present with us in the flesh. Christ is God. The Jesus of the New Testament is the Jehovah of the Old Testament. The Incarnate Word is the inspirer of the written word. Peter tells us distinctly that the prophets who spake of the grace that should come unto us, searched "what, or what manner of time, the Spirit of Christ which was in them did signify when He testified beforehand" (I Peter I. 10, 11).

Christ's words are the words of the whole Bible, and it is to them we must hearken, and them that we must obey.

How clear, and rich and comfortable they are, satisfying every human need, every yearning and every aspiration! Is it a question of guidance in our daily walk? Is it the supply of our common needs, what we shall eat and drink, and our body, "what we shall put on"? Are we longing for solace and fellowship in sorrow? Are we peering into the darkness for some trace of departed footsteps, straining our ears for some echo of voices that seem forever lost?

This is the answer to our need: "In nothing be anxious; but in everything by prayer and supplication, with thanksgiving, let your requests be made known unto God. And the peace of God, which passeth all understanding, shall guard your hearts and your thoughts in Christ Jesus." (Philippians IV. 6, 7. R.V.)

SPIRITISM IN ISRAEL AND JUDAH

I

In previous chapters it has been said that the spiritistic medium does not bring back the dead, but that the "familiar spirit" who controls the medium appears able to *personate* the dead. Satan knows very much, some would say he knows all, about the life of every human being, for he ever goes "about seeking whom he may devour." At least information could be procured with lightning speed from the demons which had watched the life of the person invoked, and then communicated to the "control" in any given case.

But while we say that the dead do not come back, it is known to readers of the Bible that some apparent exceptions must be made. Take the case of the transfiguration of Christ, when "Behold, two men talked with him, which were Moses and Elias, who appeared in glory and spake of his decease which he should accomplish at Jerusalem" (Luke IX. 30, 31).

Take the crucifixion, when "the graves were opened, and many bodies of the saints which slept arose, and came out of the graves after his resurrection, and went into the holy city and appeared unto many" (Matt. XXVII. 52, 53).

And then there were Lazarus and the son of the widow of Nain, but these are instances of the raising of the dead where there was a second occurrence of death. In the others the dead saints appeared only for a little while and then immediately vanished, not appearing again.

With the exception of Samuel of whose case this chapter treats, there is no similar record of the dead returning to this world. And in no case except his, did the dead speak to or in any other way communicate with the living.

Moses and Elijah spake with Christ but did not speak to the disciples. The saints rising at His resurrection was a special testimony to that fact. As another expresses it, "When Christ died, the graves were opened to show that there was power in His death to open the graves of believers; and when three days later, He arose, they arose with Him to show that there was power in His resurrection to bring them forth."

They appeared unto many, but so far as we know they did not speak to a single person.

II

Samuel's case is unique. Saul, the king of Israel at the time, had professedly put the necromancers out of Israel at the Divine command, being urged to do it doubtless, by Samuel himself.

But now the glittering helms and spears of an invading army surrounded him, and his heart trembled with gloomy forebodings. The Spirit of the Lord no longer came upon him, and the phantoms of past sins floated continually before his eyes taking away rest and all steadfastness of purpose. Samuel who had so long borne with and entreated for him was dead. He tried to pray, but iniquity was in his heart and the Lord would not hear him. He was answered no more neither by dreams, nor by Urim, nor by the prophets. No voice answered to his despairing cry.

Then he yielded to the evil thought, and perhaps stifling his conscience with the plea that it was a prophet of the Lord with whom he would converse, he appeals to the powers of darkness.

He asks his companions "if they knew of any surviving dealer with demons." Yes, they know of one, proof doubtless, that they had been in the habit of consulting her themselves, and in the shelter of the night Saul goes forth with two of them to a slope of Mount Hermon.

Entering into the cavern, dimly lighted by a fire of wood, and addressing the medium, he says: "I pray thee, divine unto me by the familiar spirit, and bring me him up whom I shall name unto thee."

The medium, suspicious at first, is re-assured by an oath that no harm would befall her, and being requested to call up Samuel commenced her preparations.

But the usual procedure is cut short by a sudden interference, and the medium is affrighted by her discovery, communicated through the familiar spirit no doubt, that her inquirer is the king; and still more affrighted by the apparition of a being with whom she had neither part nor lot. The explanation of this last remark is that the real Samuel had appeared instead of the personation which the medium had expected, the real Samuel, whom God, in wrath, had sent up as the bearer of a fearful message of doom to the wicked king (I Samuel XXVIII).[1]

The rest of the story we need not follow. The words of Samuel, the despair of Saul, his return to camp, his suicidal death the next day, and very especially the declaration in I Chron. X. 13, that he "died for his transgression which he committed against the Lord, * * * and for asking counsel of one that had a familiar spirit to inquire of it."

The view of Pember, thus quoted, that it was indeed the real Samuel who came up, and not a personated Samuel, is that of the present writer also, (Synthetic Studies page, 43, Christian Worker's Commentary, page 166).

But it is necessary to emphasize the point that it was not the witch of Endor who brought up Samuel. Matters got out of her hands apparently, as indicated in her screams. God brought up Samuel, and the fact that Saul saw and spoke directly to him is another feature which is uncommon in Spiritistic lore.

The incident, therefore, is a special one, and affords no evidence as to the genuineness of other communications purporting to come from individuals who have left this world. It is no proof whatever that the spirit of any particular individual can be summoned by a medium or 'control', or that the spirits which respond are those of the individuals they purport to be. (The Vital Choice: Endor or Calvary.)

And yet it is only right to say that there is another view to be taken of this transaction. It is one that gives no more comfort, perhaps not even as much, to the votaries of Spiritism, and would not be mentioned here at all, except as a matter of additional interest.

The Rev. William H. Clagett in his brochure, "Modern Spiritualism

Exposed," presents it cogently in speaking of the occurrence as the first séance of which the world has any record.

That record plainly shows, he says, that this spirit was *not* Samuel's. He thinks it came from the wrong direction, "up" not down. Again the spirit says, "Why hast thou *disquieted* me?" He does not think that any of God's servants could be disquieted by a witch. Still further, the spirit says, "Tomorrow, thou shalt be with me." Samuel was a saved man, Saul a lost man, and between the two a great impassable gulf was fixed. How could Saul be with Samuel?

Furthermore, Dr. Clagett believes that if this spirit had been Samuel he would have told Saul to repent and call upon God, instead of which he makes an argument to drive Saul to despair, declaring that God had departed from him and become his enemy, and that he would be defeated and slain, etc.

Notwithstanding what Dr. Clagett says however, and though there are others who agree with him, the simple reading of the record impresses one that the real Samuel is before us.

An answer to one of Dr. Clagett's objections, and the most serious one, is ready. The Jews regarded the place of the dead as composed of two realms, one for the righteous and one for the unrighteous. Tomorrow Saul might have been with Samuel in that he was in the realm of the dead, and yet not with him in the sense that he was in the company of the righteous dead.

Yet omitting this particular factor, we have here indeed, as Dr. Clagett says, a picture of modern Spiritism drawn by the finger of God three thousand years ago. The whole thing is laid bare before us, the medium and her character, the supposed "control", the circle, Saul and two men with him, the time, night, the claim, "whom shall I bring up?", the supposed materialization, and the same arrangement of things in the house, and the same vagueness and uncanniness about the whole proceeding.

III

After the period of Saul little is said of Spiritism in Israel until we reach the defection of Baal-worship in the time of King Ahab and the prophet Elijah (I Kings XVII-XIX); where the supposition is a reasonable one that the false prophets were mediums inspired by the agents of Satan.

For this cause, let the reader be duly impressed with the awful story in I Kings XXII, especially verses 20-23, where a lying spirit is permitted, in Divine judgment, to seduce the king so that he is led away to a disgraceful death.

Later comes the story of Naaman the leper (2 Kings V), who was indignant because God's servant Elisha did not "wave his hand over the place and recover the leper." Was he thinking of the mesmeric healing of the pagan priests? If so, it enables us to appreciate why Elisha bade him instead, to go "wash in Jordan seven times and thy flesh shall come again to thee and thou shalt be clean."

These are instances of the coupling of sorcery and idolatry in the history of the ten tribes, but the same is found in Judah too. Was it in Jotham or Ahaz' day, that Israel cried to Jehovah: "Therefore Thou hast forsaken Thy people, the house of Jacob, because they be replenished from the east, and are soothsayers like the Philistines" (II. 6)?

When a century afterwards, Manasseh is on the throne, "he did that which was evil in the sight of the Lord, after the abominations of the heathen whom the Lord cast out before the children of Israel. * * * And he made his son to pass through the fire, and observed times, and used enchantments, and dealt with familiar spirits and wizards" (2 Kings XXI).

In consequence of these practices there follows a fearful prophecy of woe. Such evil would be brought on Jerusalem and Judah as would cause the ears of him that heard of it to tingle. The city would be wiped "as a man wipeth a dish, wiping it and turning it upside down." Moreover Manasseh himself was permitted of God to be taken in chains by the king of Assyria and carried to Babylon.

Happily however, Manasseh offers an answer to the question as to whether it is ever possible for a soul entangled in Spiritism to be delivered and restored, for we read in 2 Chronicles XXIII. 12, 13, that when he was in affliction he besought the Lord his God, and humbled himself greatly before the God of his fathers, and prayed unto Him. As a result he was heard of Him Who brought him again to Jerusalem into his Kingdom. "Then Manasseh knew that the Lord He was God."

Manasseh's godly successor, Josiah, put away the abominations and removed the mediums from Judah, but they soon were permitted to return alas! as we judge by Jeremiah's denunciation of them up to the very moment almost of the Babylonian captivity.

"Hearken not ye to your prophets," he exclaims, "nor to your diviners, nor to your dreamers, nor to your mesmerizers, nor to your enchanters, which speak unto you, saying, ye shall not serve the king of Babylon. For they prophesy a lie unto you, to remove you far from your land, and that I should drive you out, and ye should perish" (XXVII. 9, 10).

The Jews learned many things as the result of their Babylonian captivity, but one thing they did not learn, and that was to put the false prophets and the diviners away from them forever. We are assured of this because of the warnings they receive in the post-captivity prophets.

It is clear also from the same source, that Spiritism will prevail among them when they return in unbelief to their own land in the day that is yet ahead. But when their King comes a second time to Zion then will He turn ungodliness away from Jacob, and they shall be freed forever from its curse. "It shall come to pass in that day, saith the Lord of hosts, that I will cut off the name of the idols out of the land, and they shall no more be remembered; and also I will cause the prophets and the unclean spirit to pass out of the land" (Zechariah XIII. 2).

---

1. Pember's, Earth's Earliest Ages.

EARLY CHRISTIANITY AND THE BLACK ART

I

So far as the Gospels are concerned, perhaps as much has been said already as our present treatment of the subject will permit. See the preceding chapters on "Satan—His Origin, History and Doom," and "Angels and Demons." But there is much in the Acts and the Epistles, and especially in the book of Revelation, that calls for particular attention.

Conybeare and Howson, and more recently, Sir William Ramsay[1] are good authority for saying that a marked fact in the society of paganism during the period covered by the Acts was the influence of magicians and soothsayers.

They were extraordinarily numerous the latter tells us, there being but few cities in the Greco-Roman world that did not possess several of them who catered to a large part of ordinary society. The more educated and thoughtful of the people believed them to be disreputable and maleficent and they warned young people against them, but this only went to prove their belief in the power they could exert.

And just as today, the people in those days resorted to magicians in the hope of procuring what they were unwilling to seek, or what they could not obtain, through prayer and acts of a purely religious character.

Religion was open and fair, but they preferred darkness and secrecy. Lovers sought charms or the means of enslaving the minds and possessing the persons of those they desired. Others sought the recovery of lost property, the cure of disease, business success or any of the thousand and one things that humanity covets. "There was a widespread and deep-seated feeling in the pagan mind, that the divine power was always ready and even desirous to communicate its will to men," and that the signs revealing that intention were visible all about for those who had eyes to see, i.e., through divination; or would be revealed to men through prophecy, i.e., oracles located at certain places which were ever ready to serve in that capacity for a given fee.

There was no class of opponents, Sir William assures us, with whom the earliest Christian apostles and missionaries were brought into collision so frequently, and whose antagonism was so obstinate and determined as the magicians.

At Samaria, at Paphos, at Philippi, and repeatedly at Ephesus, wizards of various kinds meet and are overcome by Peter and Paul. They had power, but the apostles are exhibited as always possessing more power.

Not that this is the only explanation of the attention given to such matters by the inspired historian, but rather is it for the purpose of refuting an accusation commonly brought against the Christians. The accusation was that they also, like the wizards and magicians, were maleficent and haters of the human race, practicing secret rites and abominable hidden crimes (I Peter II. 12). "There is no presbyter of the Christians that is not an astrologer, a diviner and a professional carer for people's physical condition" is the testimony of the supposed letter of Emperor Hadrian to a Roman Consul, A.D. 134.

We thus have a point of similarity with the way in which spiritists of today compare their doings and their beliefs with Christ and the Christians of the first and second centuries. As we have previously pointed out, they commit the blasphemy of speaking of Christ as a Master Medium, and affirm that the phenomena of the séances are not different in origin, in character and in their objective from the marvels which Christians know to have been wrought by the power of the Holy Spirit at the hands of the first disciples.

Whereas the authorities of that day sought to dishonor those marvels by reducing them to the level of unlawful arts, so the practitioners of those arts today are seeking to elevate them to the plane of the holy and divine religion of Jesus Christ.

II

As we come to consider the record of the Acts, let the reader refresh his recollection by a perusal of the text.

Take the story of Simon Magus for example, VIII. 5-24. Still following Ramsay who has an original way of looking at the matter, it is to be borne in mind that Simon was not an impostor or a quack, just as we have seen that some, a very few perhaps, of the modern mediums are not to be so designated. He possessed real power, as do some of these, though it may be of a different kind from that which he possessed.

The Samaritans said, "This man is that power of God, which is called Great" (R.V.). "Power" (Greek, *dunamis*) was what the pagan devotees worshipped as divine. "Great" also had a strong religious characteristic. Hence in Simon they thought they had "an epiphany of that Supreme power of which even the gods themselves are only partial embodiments."

But Simon saw in Philip greater and different power from any that he possessed. The powers of this world always recognize the true power of God (James II. 19). Struck with astonishment at the position and influence acquired by Philip, he joined his company to learn more about it; and on discovering through Peter and John that it was to be procured and even passed on to others by the laying on of hands, he would pay for it if it could be bought.

As Ramsay carefully notes, in this first recorded collision with a practicer of magic arts, the stress is laid on his incapacity to understand the nature and character of the Christian truth. There is an essential antagonism between him and it, just as there is today between the exponents and the votaries of revived Spiritism and they who are truly witnessing for Jesus Christ. We class Simon with Spiritists, because "in such phenomena as that of Spiritism lay the powers of such magicians."

As a matter of fact not only is Simon's proposal rejected by the Apostles, and with indignation and contempt, but Simon himself is rejected.

And it was necessary thus to give strong expression to this antagonism on the first occasion, because of the analogy between certain phenomena of the magician and those of Christianity on some occasions. Take the descent of the Holy Spirit on the waiting and praying disciples, already mentioned, which took place on the day of Pentecost. The Spiritists of today do not hesitate to class that sacred scene with a modern spiritist séance—the disciples together with one accord, the sound of the rushing mighty wind filling the house, the appearance of cloven tongues!

It is characteristic of Luke's method of correcting this erroneous idea in the book of Acts, that he does not do so by obtruding any opinion or judgment of his own, but simply by setting forth the acts and words of the heaven-endued and heaven-guided apostles, which speak for themselves. Happy are we if, learned in the contents of Holy Writ, we are able to do the same against the spiritists of today, and thus, if it please God, deliver some who, without knowing it, are like Simon, "in the gall of bitterness and in the bond of iniquity."

III

From the eighth chapter of the Acts, let the reader pass if he will to the thirteenth and to the story of "Elymas the Sorcerer."

Following further the author we have named, here is the only case in the New Testament in which the natural antagonism between the Christian teacher and the magician is carried to a direct conflict and trial of strength. Bar-Jesus (Arabic, *Elymas*) pits himself against Paul and forthwith his strength is withered. "The power of the Holy Spirit, looking through the eyes of Paul, pierces him to the soul and temporarily paralyses the nervous system so far as vision is concerned"; or to quote the inspired and less round-about language of the Bible itself, "Immediately there fell on him a mist and a darkness; and he went about seeking some one to lead him by the hand."

It is pertinent to observe that Sergius Paulus, the Roman deputy or pro-consul in this case, is described as "a prudent man," i.e., a man of understanding. His prudence and understanding were exhibited surely, in calling for Barnabas and Saul that he might hear the Word of God; and afterwards in judging that the results in the case of the false prophet who withstood them, were sufficient to accredit the truth of their testimony. "When he saw what was done, he believed, being astonished at the doctrine of the Lord."

Would to God that some of those now coming under the power of the false teaching of modern Spiritism were governed by a like prudence, especially when we reflect that Paul, under the impulse of the Spirit of God, rebuked this sorcerer as one who was "full of all subtility and mischief," a "child of the devil," and an "enemy of all righteousness" who was perverting "the right way of the Lord."

It intensifies the realism of this transaction to know that Sir William Ramsay has been able to identify this deputy by the monuments of Asia Minor, and also to corroborate in a most fascinating way the allusion to his conversion to the Christian religion.

IV

Leaving the story of Bar-Jesus we come to that of the "damsel possessed with a spirit of divination" in Acts XVI.

A maid having "a spirit, a Python" is the way we find it in the margin of the Revised Version. The King James' Version is more of a comment than a translation, and destroys the instruction which the passage was intended to give. That instruction is important as proving the supernatural character of the influences that formed and guided Paganism.

As Benjamin Wills Newton says in "Reflections on the Character and Spread of Spiritualism," this "damsel" was what men now call a medium, an intermediary between themselves and the powers of darkness—a link connecting with hell whose fires shall never be quenched (Mark IX. 43-48). She had the spirit of "Pytho" that guided the Delphic oracle, and that oracle was not human, but superhuman and Satanic.

"This authoritative connection of Spiritualism with the ancient gods," says Pember, "is of peculiar importance at a time when Apollo, the god of Delphi, is re-appearing as a mighty angelic existence in poems which claim to be demoniacally inspired."

It is thus in part, that A. T. Schofield, M.D., the London neurologist and author, describes this scene:

"Look at the setting of the story. This was the first entry of Christianity into Europe, the most momentous event in its history!

"Who could discern the mighty importance of the landing of these three obscure travelers? Only two—God and the Prince of Darkness! Mere men were busy with weightier affairs—the gossip of the court at

Rome, the rising influence of Greece, and the like; and yet through the power of the message of these three men both Empires were soon to fall beneath th sway of the crucified Nazarene! The Prince of Darkness was an unseen witness of the whole occurrence, and his plans were soon made.

"Probably the very next day, on their way to the river, his emissary, suitably disguised as an 'angel of light' met them, and gave the apostle a most hearty and unexpected welcome. She evidently knew all about their arrival and their gospel, and the part in the drama she had to play.

"Ancient Spiritism was too wise to seek to discredit the Christian gospel, after the fashion of the modern variety. On the contrary, she lauded it to the skies for days, declaring it to be 'the way of salvation' and thus posed as another and a greater 'Lydia'—the true and the false were side by side. And yet the apostle was not taken in! (for the spiritual man 'discerneth all things' (I Cor. II. 15).

"How different in these times! Nowadays, if the name of God is but so much as heard at a séance, even Christians feel it is all right. While, if one of the 'soothsayers' lauded the tenets of the Christian faith after the fashion of this maid, London would ring with the news the next day as proof of the godliness of Modern Spiritism!

"It is written that the apostle was 'sore troubled,' and no wonder, with this perplexing masterpiece of the enemy, masquerading before him and undeniably preaching day after day the truth of God!

"But 'in vain is the net spread in the sight of any bird,' and Paul, instructed by the Holy Spirit and 'discerning all things,' like his Master before him (Mark I. 25, 34), refused praise from the unclean source. He saw clearly the devil that 'possessed' this pseudo-evangelist, and said to it, 'I charge thee in the name of Jesus Christ to come out of her.' He never addressed one word to the poor victim, but spoke to the real power within her.

"Are not these things written for our instruction? And is there one single soul who reads these lines so blind as not to see the parallel, or so deaf as not to hear the warning?"

V

One more incident from the Acts will suffice, the story of the Diana worshippers at Ephesus, recorded in the nineteenth chapter.

Ephesus was renowned throughout the world for the worship of Diana and the practice of magic. Mysterious symbols engraved on the image of the goddess were regarded as a charm when pronounced, and their study was an elaborate science taught in books numerous and costly.

This circumstance throws light on the peculiar character of the miracles wrought by Paul in that city, though we are not to suppose that the apostles were always able to work miracles at will, any more than we know that their miracles were not always the same.

Here he was in the face of magicians like Moses and Aaron in Egypt, and it is expressly said that his miracles were "special" or extraordinary (Acts XIX. 11).

A profound effect was produced on those who practiced curious arts in the city, and especially certain travelling exorcists who, influenced by what they had seen and heard in Paul's work, and judging also by precedent in the case of the Diana worship, supposed that the Name of Jesus acted as a charm, and attempted by such means to cast put evil spirits as the Apostle had done. "But He to whom demons were subject and Who had given to His servants power and authority over them (Luke IX. 1) had shame and terror in store for those who thus presumed to take His holy Name in vain."

Among those who thus presumed, "were seven sons of one Sceva, a Jew," "and the man in whom the evil spirit was, leaped on them so that they fled out of the house naked and wounded."

The news spread, and fear fell on the people "and the Name of the Lord Jesus was magnified," by their confession of sin and the forsaking of their evil ways, even to the extent in many cases of the burning of their costly books whose loss amounted to as much as ten thousand dollars of our money.

"So mightily grew the Word of God and prevailed" (XIX. 20).

---

1. The Bearing of Recent Discovery on the Trustworthiness of the New Testament.

TEACHING OF THE PAULINE EPISTLES

The previous chapter showed us something of the obstinate and determined antagonism of the spiritists, the sorcerers and the magicians toward the Christian apostles. But the latter met it by their inspired writings, as well as by their spoken words and the wonders and signs they wrought in the power of the Holy Spirit.

I

One of the first in the order of the books of the New Testament and one of the best known of the written words of Paul, is that in the tenth chapter of his first epistle to the Corinthians, where he says:

> "The things which the Gentiles sacrifice they sacrifice to demons and not to God; and I would not that ye should have fellowship with demons.
>
> "Ye can not drink the cup of the Lord and the cup of demons; ye can not be partakers of the Lord's table, and the table of demons.
>
> "Do we provoke the Lord to jealousy? Are we stronger than He?"

The actual existence of demons is here implied if not positively stated, as well as their actual worship by the benighted pagans. But what is more to the point so far as Christian believers are concerned, is the temptation to affiliate with such worshippers, an affiliation cutting off from communication with the true God.

And more than that, it not only severs communion, but exposes believers to the divine chastisement as implied in the words, "Do we provoke the Lord to jealousy? Are we stronger than He?" That is, will we attempt to resist His will and openly bring His honor into contempt?

The words denote the strong displeasure in consequence of adulterous love. The fiercest of all human passions is used to illustrate the hatred of God towards idolatry, and spiritist séances come dangerously near idolatry.

There is a curious passage in the eleventh chapter of the same epistle which has puzzled commentators. It is where Paul is instructing women how to behave themselves in the assemblies of worship:

> "Neither was the man created for the woman; but the woman for the man.
>
> "For this cause ought the woman to have power on her head because of the angels."

One of the commentators consulted in the preparation of this chapter, added, "for some remarkable Oriental illustrations of the interpretation that evil angels are here meant, see Dean Stanley on this verse."

An examination of Dean Stanley, with whose commentary the present writer had not previously been particularly acquainted, revealed that he favored the view of Kurtz, Maitland, Fleming and others as to the Angel interpretation of Genesis VI. referred to in previous chapters; and that he connected this admonition of Paul with the extraordinary event there named.

His words, in part, follow, and are given somewhat at length because of their bearing on what has gone before:

> "The apostle had dwelt on the necessity of this subordination, as shown in all the passages in the early chapters of Genesis, where the relation of the sexes is described, viz. Gen. 1.26, II. 18, 23, III. 16.
>
> "The mention of these passages may have carried on his thoughts to the next and only kindred passage in Gen. VI. 2, 4, in which those relations are described as subverted by the union of the

daughters of men with the sons of God, —in the version of the LXX. the *angels*.

"In this case the sense would be In this subordination of the woman to man, we find the reason of the custom, which, in consequence of the sin of the angels, enjoins that the woman ought not to part with the sign that she is subject, not to them, but to her husband. The authority of the husband is, as it were, enthroned visibly upon her head, in token that she belongs to him alone, and that she owes no allegiance to any one besides, not even to the angels who stand before the throne of God"

"The 'fall of the angels' thus spoken of is the same as that indicated in Jude 6, 2 Pet. II. 4, where the context shows that the fall there intended is supposed to be at the time not of the creation, but of the Deluge, not from pride but lust.

"It is possible that, if the words 'on account of the angels' be so taken, the word 'power' might be understood, not as the sign of the husband's power over the woman, but (in the sense most agreeable to the usage of the word itself) as the sign of the power or dignity of the woman over herself, protecting her from the intrusion of spirits, whether good or evil. In that case compare its use in VII. 37.

"Finally, we must ask why a train of argument, otherwise simple, should be thus abruptly interrupted by allusions difficult in themselves, and rendered still more so by their conciseness?

"The most natural explanation seems to be that he was led by a train of association familiar to his readers, but lost to us. Such is the allusion in 2 Thess. II. 5, 6, 'Remember ye not, that, when I was yet with you, I told you these things? And now ye know what withholdeth,' etc.

"An argument in their letter, a conversation, a custom to which he had before alluded, would account not only for the introduction of the passage, but for allusions which, as addressed merely to a local or transitory occasion, might well be couched in terms so obscure as to forbid in effect, if not in design, any certain or permanent inference from them for future ages.

"The difficulty of the text is, in fact, the safeguard against its misuse."

This church to which it was necessary to say so much about evil spirits, was one which, perhaps more than any other, had abused the spiritual gifts bestowed upon it by the Holy Spirit for the propagation of the Gospel. Hence the large place given to spiritual gifts in this epistle, covering chapters XII-XIV.

These chapters challenge the most prayerful consideration in connection with our theme, touching as they do, the source of such gifts (XII. 4-6); their nature (7- 11); their object and use (12-31); the cause of their abuse (XIII. 1-13); the preference among them, and why (XIV. 1-25); the manner in which they are to be publicly exercised (26-35); and indeed everything else required for their wise and holy employment in the blessing of men and the extension of the knowledge of the true God and our Saviour Jesus Christ.

II

Galatians comes next in order after Corinthians with its warning against idolatry and sorcery (V. 20) placing them alongside of adultery, fornication and all uncleanness in the catalogue of the works of the flesh. "Idolatry is the open recognition of false gods," says Lightfoot, "and sorcery the secret tampering with the powers of evil." They are like the two halves of one whole. "They which do (practice R.V.) such things," the apostle admonishes, "shall not inherit the Kingdom of God" (21).

It is not said, "they that do such things daily," for even though one does any such thing even only once, voluntarily, he forfeits the kingdom of God as long as he remains under the dominion of that work of the flesh.—Starke.

A plainer and more fearful notice of danger to the necromancers of the present day it would be impossible to put into words.

III

Paul's letter to the Ephesians follows with a revelation of the conflict in which Christian believers are engaged in this matter, together with a description of the protection to be taken and the weapon to be used for victory and the assurance of its attainment if the command be obeyed.

Beginning with the tenth verse of the sixth chapter, he says:

"Finally, my brethren, be strong in the Lord and in the power of His might.

"Put on the whole armour of God, that ye may be able to stand against the wiles of the devil.

"For we wrestle not against flesh and blood, but against principalities, against powers, against the rulers of the darkness of this world, against spiritual wickedness in high places."

"Wrestle" indicates a personal encounter, a contest of life and death. But it is not one with "flesh and blood"; it is not against humanity viewed in its palpable characteristics that we wrestle, but with spirits high in rank and position. As Dr. Eadie says, "it is no vulgar herd of fiends we encounter, but such of them as are darkly eminent in place and dignity."

Moreover they are "the rulers of the darkness of this world," those which in some way, and for some reason, "have acquired a special domination on earth, out of which they are loath to be dislodged." This "darkness," to quote him further, is that "spiritual obscurity which so painfully environs the church—that zone which surrounds an unbelieving world with an ominous and lowering shadow." No wonder we should take unto us "the whole armour of God," not a part, but the whole.

Dropping the figures which Paul uses in the subsequent verses, the protection and the weapon that he names and which we all need, are truth, righteousness, peace, faith, salvation, the Word of God and prayer.

"Truth" here is subjective, it is "the assured conviction that we believe and that it is God's truth that we believe." The intimate dealing of truth with the soul, "the affections and judgment braced up to Christ and the things of Christ."

The "righteousness" also is subjective. It is not the imputed righteousness of Christ, and which is presupposed as the possession of the believer, but the practical every day righteousness growing out of it, the "good conscience" which Peter repeatedly urges upon those to whom he writes.

The same is true of "peace". It is peace as an experience, the effect of maintaining a good conscience. The Christian warrior moves as the battle shifts, and his continued preparedness for action, his feet shod, depends on that serenity of heart which nothing perplexes or disconcerts.

"Faith" in God and His grace is needed also to "guard the mind from aberration and despondency, and ward off the assaults that are made upon it."

"Salvation" in this instance means the conscious possession, the knowledge of safety, the conviction of pardon and sanctification. He who thus knows that he has passed from death unto life is one whose "head is covered in the day of battle."

As "the helmet of salvation" crowns the various parts of the armor, so there comes after it no reference to any further means of defence, which is quite complete, but a revelation of the instrument of offensive energy against the adversary, "the sword of the Spirit which is the Word of God."

And then the hidden spring of power without which nothing avails, "praying always." But always in the Spirit, i.e. the Holy Spirit, in His exciting and assisting influence (Romans VIII. 26, Jude 20). "And watching thereunto," watching for these very things thus specified to be realized in us, and in "all the saints."

IV

We pause in Colossians to point out its teaching concerning evil spirits in their relation to the Person and work of Christ in our redemption (chapter II. 13-15).

We who were "dead in trespasses and sins" have been quickened together with Him Who blotted out the handwriting of ordinances that was against us, and took it out of the way, nailing it to His Cross;

> "And having spoiled principalities and powers He made a show of them openly, triumphing over them in it",

i.e. in His cross.

Nicholson (Oneness With Christ) renders it: "Stripping off and away from Himself the principalities and powers, He made a show of them boldly, leading them in triumph in it."

The evil principalities and powers are here meant of course, the same as in Ephesians VI. 12. They seized on Christ's human nature, which, though without sin, had infirmities, as we saw illustrated in the wilderness temptation, and the agony of Gethsemane as well as Calvary. But His victory was complete, for the powers of evil which had thus clung to Him were turned off and cast away forever by His death and resurrection.

And yet there is a higher or, if you please, a deeper view to be taken of this truth. The evil principalities and powers attacked our Lord on His spiritual side as well.

Satan did this in the wilderness, in seeking to keep Him from the cross by offering Him "the kingdoms of the world and the glory of them" if he would fall down and worship him (Matthew IV). And the same temptation came to Him from the same source at other times and in other ways. When Peter sought to dissuade Him from going up to Jerusalem to be killed was such a time (Matthew XVI. 21), and when the Greeks desired to see Him at the feast, and learning of it, He exclaimed, "Now is My soul troubled, and what shall I say? Father, save me from this hour." John XII. 27.)

But He was not rebellious, neither turned He away backward. He set His face like a flint and He knew that He should not be ashamed (Isa. L). He died, but He arose again. So pleasing to His Father was the substitution of Himself for sinners and so absolute and glorious His defeat of the dire purposes of Satan, sin, death and all the powers of darkness, that the cross itself became the victor's car.

To quote Bishop Wilson in his Lectures on Colossians,

"At the very moment when Satan and the Jews conceived that they had accomplished their hellish purpose; when Christ and His new religion seemed crushed at a blow; when the efforts of the evil one which had succeeded against the first Adam appeared to succeed against the Second Adam; when the sun veiled in darkness might be thought to symbolize the destruction of man's expectations of redemption excited during 4,000 years—at that very instant, behold the triumph!

"The law fulfilled; God's moral government vindicated; death robbed of its prey; Satan dethroned from his usurped position; principalities and powers led in procession as captives, and a show openly made of them before a rescued world!"

Where, then, are the inventions and follies of men? Where the worship of principalities and powers? Do not spiritists see the peril of the company they keep, and do not Christians rejoice in the comfort and protection of that Mighty One on Whom help has been laid, and under the shadow of Whose wings they have come to trust?

V

In his first epistle to the Thessalonians (II. 18), Paul charges the devil by name as the opposer of his work, in a passage parallel to that of the inspired Chronicler "and Satan stood up against Israel" (I Chron. XXL 1).

The Apostle had endeavored to go back from Athens to visit the afflicted brethren at Thessalonica, "but Satan hindered us." The hindrance exhibits itself to the reader of Acts 17 as the persecuting Jews, but the spiritually illumined Apostle sees not "flesh and blood," but "the rulers of the darkness of this world," Satan and the evil angels whom he directs. He also was the tempter of the Thessalonian Christians themselves, in whom, because of their tribulation, there was danger that Paul's labor might be in vain.

This leads up to the larger consideration of the occult powers in the second epistle, where at the second chapter, the writer is dealing with the apostasy already at work in the Church, and the development of that wicked or lawless one (the Antichrist).

This being is identified as one

> "Whose coming is after the working of Satan with all power, and signs and lying wonders, and with all deceivableness of unrighteousness in them that are perishing because they received not the love of the truth, that they might be saved."

These "lying wonders" are so called, not because they are not real wonders which Satan and his emissaries are able to do, but because they are done in the interest of and to bolster up a lie. Their seriousness lies in the fact that they are wrought "with all deceit of unrighteousness." But note that it is only "them that are perishing" (R.V.) on whom the deceit works, them that have "not the love of the truth that they might be saved."

The "truth" means of course, the gospel of Jesus Christ, and as the present writer has sought to show in his Antidote to Christian Science, there is a difference between receiving the truth and receiving the love of it. A man who marries a woman without loving her is soon seeking a divorce, and he who knows the truth in his head, but has never given it lodgment in his heart, is not difficult to lead into error.

But the momentous feature of this is that, as the subsequent verses in the chapter show, because men receive not the love of the truth God sends upon them as a judgment, a "working of error," a "strong delusion that they should believe a lie." It is not merely that God permits such a delusion to come upon them, but that He sends it as the mighty act of a Judge punishing evil by evil.

Not to believe the truth of the gospel is sin, and not to receive the love of it after knowing it is still deeper sin; but to be obliged to believe a lie in consequence of it is retribution unspeakable. The Greek in this case might be translated "THE lie," as the idea is not merely a single lie, but the entire force of lies, the entire element of the devilish perversion of all truth (Auberlen in loco).

VI

The last of the Pauline utterances on the subject of which we shall now treat is in I Timothy IV., and is distinguished from all the preceding as a prediction of the increase of demoniacal influence in the latter days, upon which many students of the Bible consider that we are now entering. The passage is part of that which concludes the preceding chapter, and we quote it with that context:

> "And, without controversy, great is the mystery of godliness; God (or 'He, Who', R.V.) was manifest in the flesh, justified in the Spirit, seen of angels, preached unto the Gentiles, believed on in the world, received up into glory.
>
> "Now (or 'But', R.V.) the Spirit speaketh expressly that in the latter times some shall depart from the faith, giving heed to seducing spirits, and doctrines of demons;
>
> "Speaking lies in hypocrisy; having their conscience seared with a hot iron;
>
> "Forbidding to marry, and commanding to abstain from meats, which God hath created to be received with thanksgiving of them which believe and know the truth."

The key to the interpretation of this remarkable passage is the words, "depart from the faith." The object, or more properly, the essence of the faith is that great Mystery of the Lord Jesus Christ spoken of in the first verse quoted, and which is at once the source and the support of all real godliness.

The departure from the faith, the apostasy as it is described in II. Thessalonians 2, is to commence with a waning faith in Christ, His Person and His work, as set forth in the Scriptures. As Pember says, "it is not necessarily a total denial of Him, but it begins with incredulity as to the miraculous circumstances of His past advent, and so gradually obscures the only source and centre of every godly aspiration." In other words, it is precisely what we are witnessing today throughout Christendom, and which furnishes a reason, in part, for believing that these are the "latter times."

The "latter times" do not mean the end of the world by any means, but the end of the present age, or dispensation, when God has been dealing in grace with sinners, and offering them a free salvation through His Son.

"The Spirit speaketh expressly that in the latter times some shall depart from the faith." The Holy Spirit is meant in this case, Who spoke expressly, or plainly, in the Old Testament prophets, through Jesus Christ Himself, and also by Paul (Daniel VII. 25; VIII. 23; Matthew XXIV. 1124; 2 Thess. II. 3).

What the Spirit says is that in the latter times some will "depart from the faith giving heed to seducing spirits and doctrines of demons." These "spirits" would be working in and through the heretical teachers, and their doctrine, or teaching, would be that of demons, Satan's ministers.

They would speak "lies in hypocrisy" or through the hypocrisy of lying teachers, the feigned sanctity of the seducers or deceivers, "having their own conscience seared." That is to say, "austerity would gain for them a show of sanctity while preaching false doctrine," they would professedly be leading others to holiness while their own conscience was defiled. It would be seared as with a hot iron, cauterized, the effect of which is to produce insensibility.

In the words of Canon Faussett, "sensuality leads to false spiritualism," hence these hypocritical teachers would make moral perfection consist in abstinence from outward things, chiefly two, "forbidding to marry and commanding to abstain from meats."

"From these last particulars," says Pember, "many have endeavored to fasten this prophecy upon the Church of Rome, because she forbids her priests to marry, and has set apart days for fasting". But Paul teaches that those of whom he speaks would receive their doctrines from wandering spirits, for the word "seducing" is capable of that rendering (compare Job I. 7; II. 2; Matthew XII. 43)."

Moreover the prohibition of marriage in this case is general, not limited to "priests" or Christian ministers, apparently an entire repudiation of God's ordinance; while the command to abstain from meats, likewise means a total, not an occasional or periodical, abstinence from certain kinds of food, of which more later on.

Meanwhile, a further remark of Canon Faussett is pertinent, viz., that "Rome's Judaizing elements will ultimately be combined with the open, worldly-wise anti-Christianity of the false prophet or beast" (VI. 20, 21; Rev. XIII. 12-15). In Spiritism instructing demons are sometimes introduced with flaming crosses in their hands, and its doctrine of the seven spheres closely approaches the Romish teaching about Purgatory.

Indeed Spiritism is nothing but a revival of the influence which originated Paganism, while Romanism as a system though it contains much truth, is only Paganism under a veil, so that the ultimate amalgamation of the two presents no insuperable difficulty.

It remains to mention that Spiritism meets the two-fold prediction, "forbidding to marry and commanding to abstain from meats." It propagates the first by the prohibition of marriage altogether, and also by "strange doctrines of elective affinities and spiritual alliances, which tend to an utter rejection of marriage as ordained by God."

As to the second, it has always been recognized that abstinence from a flesh diet is indispensable to great mediumistic power, to say nothing of the doctrine of transmigration of souls which, from being a tenet of Theosophy, is now finding favor with the Spiritistic school.

The limits of our present task forbid an enlargement on these points, but the interested reader is directed to Pember's Earth's Earliest Ages, Spiritualism, Part III., and to the Bibliography on the subject which he names.

TEACHING OF THE GENERAL EPISTLES

I

There is an added attraction to the study of our subject in the General Epistles because they bring before us again, and from a different point of view, the mystery of the fallen angels dealt with earlier.

This is done in I Peter III. 19, which speaks of Christ preaching to "the spirits in prison." At that point the inspired writer is using the example of Christ to encourage and comfort Christian believers in their suffering for righteousness' sake, saying:

> "For Christ also hath once suffered for sins, the just for the unjust, that he might bring us to God, being put to death as to the flesh, but quickened as to the spirit:
>
> "By which also he went and preached unto the spirits in prison."

The words "spirits in prison" have sometimes been employed to teach the false doctrine of the "second chance" or a probation after death. In such cases the theory is advanced that Christ went into the place of the wicked dead and preached the gospel to them giving them another opportunity to believe and be saved.

If this were indeed the teaching of the passage, every true Christian preacher surely, would wish to proclaim it; but aside from the fact that it is taught in no other place in the Bible it certainly is not taught here.

For example, the Greek word for "preached" in this instance is not that which the New Testament commonly employs for the preaching of the Gospel, but a different word. It means to proclaim after the manner of a herald. Grimm, the philologist, quoted by E. W. Bullinger, says that the word is always used with a suggestion of formality and an authority which must be listened to and obeyed.

Moreover, if the subject of the proclamation is not clearly implied in the context of this word when it is used, then it must be distinctly stated if we are to know what it is. That is to say, if it is the proclamation of the Gospel that is intended, then the word "Gospel" must be used to insure that application, which is not the case here.

In the next place, the word "spirits" does not apply to men. It is never so applied in the Bible when it stands alone and without any qualifying words, as it does here. A possible exception is Hebrews XII. 23, but there it is expressly said that "the spirits of just men" are meant, "the spirits of just men made perfect." As Bullinger says, "man was made, and up to the time of his death he continues to be, a 'living soul'." It is so also after death (Revelation VI. 9; XX. 4) and until the resurrection, when the word "spirit" is used as a brief term for man's spiritual body (I Cor. XV. 45).

But the word "spirits" by itself and without any qualifying description is used always of supernatural beings, higher than man and lower than God. When there is any doubt as to the kind of spirit referred to, some defining word is employed like "unclean spirits," "evil spirits," etc. The defining words in this case are "spirits in prison," very evidently therefore, evil spirits.

But do we inquire just what evil spirits are meant, the nature of their offence and the time of its perpetration? The information is furnished in the next verse, where we are told that they were those

> "Which aforetime were disobedient, when once the longsuffering of God waited in the days of Noah, while the ark was a preparing, wherein few, that is, eight souls were saved by water."

Very clearly this points back to the record in the sixth chapter of Genesis, and recalls what was considered previously as to the fallen angels and the "sons of God" marrying the "daughters of men."

There remains therefore only the inquiry as to what it was that Christ went thus and proclaimed to them in prison? The answer to which is found in the particular purpose of this epistle, which is to comfort Christian believers under persecution for righteousness' sake, and to encourage and strengthen them in their witness bearing for Christ.

In other words, Peter is here using the example of Christ in that connection. He suffered and died as to His flesh, but He was quickened as to His spirit, that is to say, He had a glorious resurrection in a spiritual body. And He had more than this, He had a glorious triumph also! God raised Him from the dead and gave Him glory (I. 21).

So complete was this triumph, and so far-reaching the proclamation of it, that it extended even to the spirits in prison. He "spoiled principalities and powers and made a show of them openly" (Col. II. 15). "And He is now gone into heaven, and is on the right hand of God, angels and principalities and powers being made subject unto Him" (III. 22).

II

The thought is carried forward in Peter's second epistle at chapter two.

False prophets are there being warned against "whose judgment now of a long time lingereth not and their damnation (or destruction) slumbereth not."

> "For if God spared not the angels that sinned, but cast them down to hell, and delivered them into chains of darkness, to be reserved unto judgment;
>
> "And spared not the old world, but saved Noah the eighth person, a preacher of righteousness, bringing in the flood upon the world of the ungodly;
>
> "And turning the cities of Sodom and Gomorrah into ashes condemned them with an overthrow, making them an example unto those that after should live ungodly;
>
> "And delivered just Lot, vexed with the filthy conversation of the wicked.
>
> * * * * * *

"The Lord knoweth how to deliver the godly out of temptation, and to reserve the unjust unto the day of judgment to be punished:

"But chiefly them that walk after the flesh in the lust of uncleanness, and despise government."

What angels are here referred to? Are they those who fell with Satan anterior to the creation of man, or those spoken of, as we before showed, in Genesis VI, just prior to the flood?

If the former, why is not Satan mentioned with them? As Kurtz remarks, "whenever else allusion is made to the tempter and those who were associated with him in his fall, mention is expressly made of Satan, and for the most part, of him only."

That it should be otherwise in this place is the more remarkable because it is Peter's aim to show that God punishes not only men who sin, like these false prophets, but beings who are the most eminent in rank. If therefore he had in mind a reference to the angels who fell at the first with Satan, would he not have named the latter, the chiefest and the leader of the apostates?

But to quote Fleming once more, a still stronger argument that the angels before the flood are meant, is found in the fact that they have been "cast down to hell (Tartarus) and delivered into chains of darkness to be reserved unto judgment."

This is not the state of Satan and his angels since the fall, for they are still permitted to move through the world, and to tempt and overcome those men who are not arrayed in the armor of God (Job I. 7; Eph. V. 12; I Pet. V. 8). Moreover, as if to preclude all doubt upon the subject, it is declared in Rev. XX. that Satan shall *hereafter* be chained, evidently therefore, he is not chained now.

The argument might be pressed further; for if the angels who sinned before the flood are not meant, why the allusion to the flood and the salvation of Noah in the next verse, the same as in I Pet. III. 19?

Nor should it escape the reader that there is significance in the reference to Sodom and Gomorrah in verse 6, and "chiefly them that walk after the flesh in the lust of uncleanness, and despise government," in verse 10. The correspondence between these illustrations or examples and the conduct of the angels before the flood is too striking to be overlooked.

III

The subject is continued in Jude verses 4-8, which closely resemble those just quoted from Peter, so closely indeed as to preclude "all idea of entire independence." Some commentators suppose that Jude wrote the earlier of the two, and that Peter copied from him, omitting or adding under the guidance of the Holy Spirit, as suited his purpose.

However this may be, it is evident that both writers refer to the same apostasy of angels, and that it is the one identified as taking place just before the flood.

To the arguments above stated in proof of this, might be added one founded on the use by New Testament writers of the term "angels," which word, when used by itself, is never employed to denote the spirits who fell at the beginning with Satan. These are spoken of as "demons," just as their head is spoken of as "the devil" or "Satan".

Kurtz, who uses this argument, admits that there are some places which seem to contradict it, but their critical examination proves otherwise. It is his conclusion that "as the apostles have employed the naked term, neither they themselves intended, nor would their first readers have been likely to perceive, an allusion to the fall of Satan and his angels."

A close exegesis of Jude confirms this opinion. His design was to guard believers against the corrupt principles and the licentious practices of certain men whom he describes as "turning the grace of God into lasciviousness," and, as one of the old divines expresses it, "his whole discourse is pointedly and especially directed against that particular sin."

He therefore reminds them of the earlier instances in which that sin had brought down divine judgment. In the case of Israel for example, the angels, inhabitants of Sodom and Gomorrah and those of the cities round about them. "In like manner," or "in like manner to these" had they given "themselves over to fornication going after strange flesh."

The phrase "in like manner," or "in like manner to these" does not refer to the ungodly men nor to Sodom and Gomorrah, as some have supposed, but to the angels, for which we have the strong authority of Dean Alford, who says the manner of the sin of these cities was similar, "because the angels committed fornication with another race than themselves, thus also going after strange flesh." He names several other Greek scholars and Bible exegetes as holding the same view.

IV

We conclude this chapter with a reference to I John IV. 1-3:

> "Beloved, believe not every spirit, but try the spirits whether they are of God: because many false prophets are gone out into the world.
>
> "Hereby know ye the Spirit of God: Every spirit that confesseth that Jesus Christ is come in the flesh is of God:
>
> "And every spirit that confesseth not that Jesus Christ is come in the flesh is not of God: and this is that spirit of antichrist, whereof ye have heard that it should come; and even now already is it in the world."

It may be doubted whether the word "spirits" in verse I has the objective application we have heretofore given to it. That is, we are not sure that John is now speaking of evil spirits, or demons, with an independent existence from the experience or thought of the prophets, but rather of the mental state, or the nature of the prophets themselves. Or to express it in another way, it is not a "familiar spirit" who controls the "medium" that is here in mind, but the medium's own spirit.

And yet there is a close relation between the two, and what the inspired apostle has to teach us about the spirits of the "false prophets" is to the point.

In Neander's expository lectures on this book, he observes that the point of transition at chapter four lies in what John had just said about the influence of the Holy Spirit in the lives of Christian believers, an influence which is the pledge of continued fellowship with Christ. In John's day much was falsely claimed to be from the Holy Spirit, just as is the case today in the teaching of Spiritism, and hence the apostle directs attention to the difference between His operations and the deceptive imitation of them.

Every spirit was not to be believed, but the spirits were to be tried as to whether they were of God. And the touchstone of the matter, the criterion by which they were to be tried was the Person and work of our Lord Jesus Christ.

Did these false spirits confess Him, i.e., did they openly acknowledge and proclaim Him? Did they confess Him as Jesus, the Christ? Not a Christ, not one out of many, but the promised one and the only one? Did they confess Him as having come in the flesh? Was He to them "the Eternal Logos in His humanization? The Divine Life-fountain letting itself down into human nature and revealing itself in visible human form—the Divine and the human in harmonious union?"

Note particularly the words, "is come" in verse 20. It is the Greek perfect, which implies not a mere past historical fact, as would be the case if another tense were used, but a present continuance of the fact and its blessed effects.

"Is come *in the flesh,*" or "clothed with flesh." Christ's was not a mere *seeming* humanity, as some have erroneously taught, but a *real* humanity. And it is necessary to believe and confess this, in order to express the truth of the atonement for sin. Only by assuming our flesh could Christ die "the just for the unjust," to bring us to God. "To deny the reality of His flesh is to deny His love, and so cast away the root which produces all true love on the believer's part" (see verses 9-11 of this same chapter).

Now every spirit that does not so confess Jesus Christ is not of God, or as some authorities render verse 3, every spirit that "annulleth" Jesus Christ is not of God. And that is just what Spiritism does. It "annulleth" Jesus Christ, the Jesus Christ of the Bible is Whom we mean. Spiritism may speak of Jesus and of Christ, but it is not "Him of whom Moses in the law, and the prophets, did write" (John I. 45).

In proof of this, we referred in our first chapter to Basil King's book, and now we would add something from Sir A. Conan Doyle's, "The New Revelation":

> "Let us look at the light we get from the spirit guides on this question of Christianity," he says. "Opinion is not absolutely uniform yonder any more than it is here, but reading a number of messages upon this subject, they amount to this:
>
> "That there are many higher spirits with our departed. They vary in degree. Call them 'angels', and you are in touch with the old religious thought.
>
> "High above all these is the greatest spirit of whom they have cognizance—not God, since God is so infinite that He is not within their ken—but one who is nearer God and to that extent represents God. This is the Christ-spirit.
>
> "His special care is the earth. He came down upon it at a time of great earthly depravity in order to give people, the lesson of an ideal life. Then he returned to his own high station, having left an example which is still occasionally followed.

"That is the story of Christ as the spirits have described it. There is nothing here of Atonement or Redemption. But there is a perfectly feasible and reasonable scheme, which I for one could readily believe." (Pp. 74, 75).

Observe that according to this teaching Christ is not God, but only represents Him as being nearer to Him than other spirits—the very error with which Paul deals in his epistle to the Colossians.

Observe also that Christ came down to the earth not as a sacrifice for sin, in Spiritism there is "nothing of atonement or redemption," but simply as an example "to give people the lesson of an ideal life."

"People can see no justice in a vicarious sacrifice, nor in a God Who could be placated by such means," says Sir Arthur. "Never was there any evidence for a fall. But if there were no fall, then what became of the atonement, of redemption from original sin, and of a large part of the Christian mystical philosophy?

"It is no uncommon thing to die for an idea," he goes on to say. "Men die continually for their convictions. Therefore the death of Christ, beautiful as it is in the Gospel narrative, has assumed an undue importance."

As to the life of Christ, Sir Arthur tells us it was lived simply in order to afford men an ideal. "Christ," he says, was "full of easy tolerance for others." He occasionally lost His temper indeed, but He was ever ready to sweep aside texts and forms and "get at the spirit of religion" (p. 72). What blasphemy!

To the same purport, the transfiguration of Christ, according to this same apostle of Spiritism, was a "story of the materialization of the two prophets upon the mountain"; and the three tabernacles suggested by Peter were three "cabinets," in other words, "the ideal way of condensing power and producing materializations"!

Such is the attitude of the New Revelation towards Christ, and the apostle John says that "this is the spirit of Anti-Christ." The Anti-Christ when he comes will be a person in human flesh, a despot, political, ecclesiastical or both, who will arise in Christendom, and whom men will worship instead of God. But his spirit, the teaching that prepares the way for his full development, is already in the world, and Spiritism is an integral part of it.

It is comforting indeed to hear John say further, addressing true believers in the Lord:

"Ye are of God, little children, and have overcome them: because greater is he that is in you, than he that is in the world.

"They are of the world: therefore speak they of the world, and the world heareth them.

"We are of God: he that knoweth God heareth us; he that is not of God heareth not us. Hereby know we the spirit of truth, and the spirit of error."

They that are of God are those who have confessed Jesus Christ in the manner John has indicated; and they have overcome the false prophets, or the lying spirits, in that they have not been brought into spiritual bondage by them. These spirits are of the world, in harmony with its feelings and opinions, therefore "the world heareth them," runs after them, and fills the air with its din.

But they that are of God heareth us; and hereby, i.e., by their confessing or not confessing Jesus Christ, know we the Spirit that comes from God and teaches truth, and the spirit that comes from Satan and is error.

TEACHING OF THE APOCALYPSE

I

In another place the present writer has mentioned twenty-five reasons why "the man of God," the true believer on Jesus Christ, should read and study the Apocalypse, or the book of Revelation, with avidity.

Among the reasons are these: (1), It describes the judgments that shall be visited upon the earth after the Church is translated; (2) it witnesses to the deliverance of certain classes of people out of those judgments; (3) it mentions particular wonders which the Church and the world shall behold in those days; (4) it traces the rise and development of the anti-christ; (5) it predicts and describes the battle of Armageddon; (6) it demonstrates the overthrow of the present world systems; (7) it portrays the Second Coming of Christ; (8) it reveals Satan's doom; (9) it gives details of the last judgment; (10) it opens the vista of the eternal age.

The reader needs to make a distinction between the end of the world and the end of the age. The end of the world, which synchronizes with the last judgment, is doubtless a long ways off. If the writer's conception of the teaching of the prophets is correct, a whole Millennium of peace and blessing on the earth shall intervene before it takes place.

On the other hand, the end of the present age or dispensation may be very near. The Scofield Reference Bible defines age or "dispensation" as "a period of time during which man is tested in respect to obedience to some specific revelation of the will of God," and states that seven such dispensations are distinguished in Scripture.

The present age or dispensation closes with the Second Coming of Christ. (See the author's Prophecy and the Lord's Return.) This event, as we understand it, takes place in two stages, or which may be represented by two scenes of a single act. In the first, our Lord comes for His Church, which is His mystical body (Ephesians I. 22, 23), and which is translated to meet Him in the air (I Thess. IV. 16-18). In the second, He descends out of the air into the earth, or to quote the precise words of Scripture, "He shall be revealed from heaven with His mighty angels, in flaming fire taking vengeance on them that know not God, and that obey not the gospel of our Lord Jesus Christ" (2 Thess. I. 7, 8).

The culmination of wickedness at the end of this age, it is predicted, will be marked by an outburst of demonism or spiritism just as at the culmination of the ante-diluvian age. To such predictions the attention of the reader has been called from time to time and they approach a climax as we enter on the study of the Apocalypse.

Prior to entering on that study however, it is important "to be persuaded that, as Pember puts it, the great aim of" Satan in all the ages has not been the spread of absolute skepticism, but the subjugation of the world to demoniacal power. His empire, in other words, can not be completely organized till men are as obedient to demons as the latter are to the rebel principalities and powers, and these last again to their great prince. "And so the denizens of darkness are not merely stirring up an aimless revolt against God; but would fain annex the whole of our world to their orderly dominions."

Philip Mauro, in "The World and Its God," puts it in another way, when he says that Satan's plan is not the destruction or injury of the race, but its well-being rather, that is, its well-being to be achieved by the best possible results attainable *apart from* God. He is doing his best, in other words, not to drag men down, but to lift them up, but according to his own standards and ideals, and for the advancement of his own interests as opposed to God.

Such being true, it may appear strange to read of some things for which evil spirits are scheduled in the history of mankind at the close of this age, and in which Satan himself is to be engaged when he learns that his time is short.

But the reason is that his time is short, and because he is tasting the bitterness of defeat. It is because also of his malignity and his lack of scruple in subjugating the victims of his will. Nor are we to forget the plan and purpose of our righteous God, in using, or permitting the use, of these wicked beings in retribution upon those who being reprobate, have "trodden under foot the Son of God and done despite unto the Spirit of grace" (Heb. X. 29).

II

Approaching the book of Revelation, we have in the ninth chapter, beginning at the 13th verse, an account of the sounding of the sixth trumpet when the four angels are loosed "which are bound at the great river Euphrates." These angels had been "prepared for the hour, and day, and month and year that they should kill the third part of man," which seems to mean that they had been reserved for a particularly appointed moment.

In other words, following Bullinger in The Apocalypse, or The Day of the Lord, these periods do not imply the duration of the judgments; but point to the time when they shall take place. There is but one article and one preposition between the four times named, which unites them, whereas had they been repeated it would have separated them and made a period of thirteen months. The very hour, of the very day, of the very month, of the very year is thus appointed by the Judge.

Bullinger also thinks that there can be no doubt that these angels are of those described by Peter and Jude as "delivered into chains of darkness, to be reserved unto (or for) judgment." And the judgment for which they have been reserved he regards as that which takes place at the end of this age. Not only are they themselves to be judged, but they are to be the executors of God's judgments upon wicked and unbelieving men. These are the "spirits in prison," he believes, to whom the Saviour proclaimed His triumph after the resurrection (i Peter III. 19).

Why they were bound at the river Euphrates we do not know, except that there may be some connection between the abyss whence they arise and wicked old Babylon, the mother of harlots and abominations of the earth (Rev. XVII. 5). Satan began his earlier activities in the earth in that region, and there may be a reason for bringing them to a climax in the same locality. (Compare Jeremiah XLVL 4-10 R.V.)

Suddenly there appear upon the scene armies of horsemen, 200,000,000, from which it may be inferred that they are not human beings but spirits, for spirits are legion. In Isaiah XXXI. we have a warning that the horses of Egypt in which Israel would trust were "flesh and not spirit," which leads to the supposition that there may be horses that are spirit and not flesh. More than this concerning them one is unable to say, but "when God thus describes them nothing ought to be easier than to believe what He says."

The Revelation goes on to say that by these three plagues, "fire, smoke and brimstone" was the third part of men killed, but that the rest of the men who were not killed, "repented not of the works of their hands, that they should not worship demons, nor idols * * * which can neither see, nor hear nor walk.

"Neither repented they of their murders, nor of their sorceries, nor of their fornication, nor of their thefts."

It is the final and full development of what is called Spiritism which is here referred to, continues Bullinger, and which calls for the plague of the Sixth Trumpet. "Sorceries of which men did not repent," are the dealings of men with spirit agencies. No wonder that God has so solemnly warned us against them, and no wonder that such awful judgments are to be visited upon them.

It is anticipating somewhat, but it may be well to mention at this point that sorcerers shall have their part in the lake that burneth with fire and brimstone, and they shall never walk in the streets of the golden city. (Rev. XXL 3; XXII. 15.)

III

The twelfth chapter of Revelation furnishes our next illustration, which tells us at verse 7 that "there was war in heaven; Michael and his angels fought against the dragon, and the dragon fought and his angels."

There is more than one place spoken of as heaven in Scripture. Perhaps as on earth there are many countries and states, so, some think, heaven may have its different spheres; and in one of these mighty spiritual forces are here revealed as set in battle array.

Michael, described elsewhere as "one of the chief princes" and "the archangel," is also said to be the prince which standeth for the Jewish people, Israel among the nations (Dan. X. 13, 21; XII. 1; Jude 9). In this action he takes the initiative against the dragon, another name for Satan, whose dominion covers all the powers and governments of the world.

The time has now come in the Divine counsels for the great historical event of the ages, and Satan, who hitherto has had some kind of access to the heavens (Job I. and II.), is about to be cast out, and "the kingdoms of the world become the Kingdom of our God and of His Christ, and He shall reign forever and ever" (Revelation XI. 15).

But when Satan is thus cast down to the earth, his angels are cast down with him, and they soon cause men to feel the meaning of the awful utterance that follows in the prophetic warning, "Woe to the inhabitants of the earth and of the sea for the devil is come down unto you, having great wrath, because he knoweth that he hath but a short time."

Then not merely the demons, but the great angels of darkness, the principalities, the powers, and the spiritual rulers of the world maddened by the thought that they have lost their fair realms forever, and that the Lord is at hand to complete their destruction, will in their rage break through every restraint, and recklessly gratify their own evil desires (Earth's Earliest Ages, p. 391).

IV

A single illustration further will suffice, and we find it in the prediction of the battle of Armageddon in chapter XVI. beginning at verse 12.

"And the sixth angel poured out his vial upon the great river Euphrates, and the water thereof was dried up, that the way of the kings of the east might be prepared."

This gathering of the kings of the east is in order to the great battle in which the heavenly and the Satanic and earthly forces are about to be engaged, an infernal crusade against the Lord and His Anointed (Psalm II). At the sounding of the sixth trumpet we saw a vast supernatural army let loose to slay a third part of men; but here a vast human army is gathered together, the whole of which, as the context shows, will be destroyed by God.

East and West are to be reckoned from the standpoint of the

prophecy and not that of the reader, which standpoint is Palestine and Jerusalem.

"And I saw," says the revelator, "three unclean spirits like frogs come out of the mouth of the dragon (Satan), and out of the mouth of the beast (Antichrist), and out of the mouth of the false prophet." ("For the further description and identity of the false prophet, see chapter XIII. 11-18.)

"For they are the spirits of demons, working miracles, which go forth unto the kings of the earth and of the whole world, to gather them to the battle of that great day of God Almighty." (Compare I Kings XXII. 19-38; Joel III. 9-17.)

"And they gather them together to a place in the Hebrew tongue Armageddon (or Har-Magadon)." The name means a Mount of Megiddo, an eminence which rises up out of the plain Esdraelon in northern Palestine, a natural battlefield, where many a contest was fought in the history of Israel; a chosen place of encampment in every contest, from Nebuchadnezzar to the recent march of Allenby into Syria. Slaughter and lamentation are associated with Megiddo (Zachariah XII. 11). In Isaiah X. 28, which describes the invasion of Palestine by the Antichrist, the Septuagint version reads "Megiddo."

Having gathered the hosts of the enemy thither, the sixth vial ends, but the description of the events to take place there will be found in connection with the pouring out of the 7th vial as found in Chapter XIX. 11-18.

We conclude with the interjectional clause in this vision, which comes in as a parenthesis. It is the voice of Christ Himself, who, while the demon spirits are gathering the kings and their armies for the last great crisis of the age, exclaims:

> "Behold I come as a thief. Blessed is he that watcheth, and keepeth his garments, lest he walk naked, and they see his shame."

The words are addressed not to the Church, not to the true believers of this age, for, if our interpretation of prophecy be correct, they will ere this have been caught up to meet the Lord in the air. They are addressed to those then dwelling on the earth and passing through its tribulation, but who have not worhsipped the beast (Anti-christ) nor his image, and who have not received his mark in the foreheads.

Christ does not come upon His Church as a thief. (I Thess. V. 4;

compare also Matt. XXIV. 38-44; Luke XII. 35-40). To His Church He comes as a welcome and expected guest (I Cor. I. 7; Col. IV. 4; I Thess. I. 9, 10; 2 Tim. IV. 8; Titus II. 13; Jas. V. 8; I Pet. V. 4; I Jno. III. 2, 3; Rev. XXII. 20).

"And now, little children, abide in Him; that, when He shall appear we may have confidence, and not be ashamed before Him at His coming" (I John II. 28).

Copyright © 2024 by Alicia EDITIONS
Credits: www.canva.com; Alicia EDITIONS.
https://www.rijksmuseum.nl/en/collection/RP-P-BI-2339
Temptation of Christ by Satan, Boëtius Adamsz. Bolswert, after Abraham Bloemaert,
1590 - 1612
ISBN PAPERBACK: 9782384553051
ISBN E-BOOK: 9782384553044
All rights reserved.
No part of this book may be reproduced in any form or by any electronic or mechanical means, including information storage and retrieval systems, without written permission from the author, except for the use of brief quotations in a book review.

www.ingramcontent.com/pod-product-compliance
Lightning Source LLC
LaVergne TN
LVHW032013070526
838202LV00059B/6438